AF264817

Tshabangu Sibusiso Malvin

Stars Do Fall in *Love*

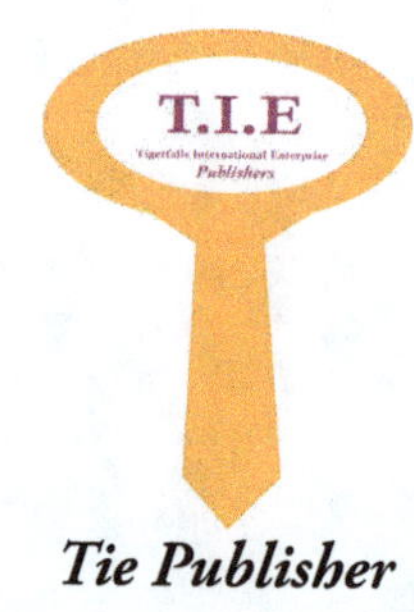

Tie Publisher

Fame

This message is for anyone who possesses a burning desire to achieve greater things in life, a desire that resides within you. The wonderful aspect of this inner drive is that it serves not only as a means to earn a livelihood but also as a powerful force that can liberate you from the confines of your past, unlocking transformative potential. Moreover, it has the remarkable ability to uncover hidden greatness within you, drawing from your accumulated knowledge and experiences. Although the path ahead may seem challenging, the ultimate value lies in the journey itself, for each of us is born with a unique purpose waiting to be discovered within ourselves.

We have just a single chance to step into the spotlight, and whatever actions you choose to undertake will forever shape your reputation and define your identity.

Table of Contents

Foreword

Fame is a way to become known and appreciated for your talents and to confidently express yourself in public. However, being famous is more complex than it may seem. When you embark on a journey of self-discovery or greater understanding, something inside you transforms. You start to perceive the world differently, and this transformation might lead to a deep appreciation for the world and everything in it. It can make you realize that even though life may have been challenging in the past, you've discovered a means to communicate effectively with others and be understood.

Many challenges could have arisen when you didn't fully understand who you are and why it's crucial to become the person you aspire to be. You searched for your true self in the wrong places, and your life experiences greatly influenced your outlook. To grow, you may have to surpass the boundaries of your current understanding. Often, our perspective is quite narrow, and we tend to mistakenly believe that the world is welcoming and that achieving your goals is a straightforward task.

When you concentrate intensely on the things that matter to you personally, there may come a point where you momentarily disregard the external world. During this time, you zero in on what you believe is the most crucial task to undertake at that very moment. As you persist in pursuing your most cherished activities, you might find yourself becoming engrossed in them, fostering an awareness that longs to connect with everything around you. In that instance, you may inadvertently lose sight of the path you once followed to harness your strength and vitality in order to make sense of life. This is how we can inadvertently stray into the realm of what used to be and grapple with the inevitable reality of the present.

Many times, you may have spent your time engaging in a hobby. It might have taken a while for you to realize that this hobby could actually become something very significant in defining who you are. We often remain at this level before everything becomes beautiful, and it unquestionably stays with us for a long time. If you never discover something truly worthwhile to dedicate your efforts to, you might later find that it has become the only thing you're familiar with.

Have you ever stopped to think about the potential hidden within you? Sometimes, we pause and question ourselves, wondering if we truly understand our purpose or if we're merely idling away our precious time. It's essential to reflect on how we invest our time and whether we're striving to excel in our pursuits. Consider the possibility that what you're currently engaged in might be the only thing you become proficient at if you don't explore other avenues.

Some individuals manage to discover a more meaningful path aligned with their life's desires instead of solely pursuing stardom or acquiring knowledge through self-guided efforts. They recognize the potential to transform a once-regarded hobby into a remarkable creation that shapes their life, a feat not everyone achieves. This realization stems from placing trust in one's own abilities.

How can you be sure that the time you've spent cannot offer you another chance to find happiness within yourself? It appears to have been a phase when you were not fully prepared to become what you genuinely aspire to be. It may feel like a shadowy stretch in your journey, where you find yourself at a crossroads between two different worlds. One path leads ahead into what you've shaped through your experiences and comprehension, while the other leads backward to a place where you aim to make amends for everything you've evolved into.

Imagine being at the very starting point of your journey. It's crucial to feel confident and content about where you're heading, even though it might not always be possible to fix all the challenges that time throws your way in just a single day. Occasionally, our inner selves call upon us to have a little more faith in our actions and endeavors because the path ahead isn't always smooth. It can take us to places we've never experienced before. Each step we take leads to another, and every door that opens reveals a new opportunity. So, as you continue through life, remember that if you don't invest in yourself, you may remain lost forever.

Initially, you may have struggled to grasp the necessity of putting in effort to attain a level where you surpass your own comprehension. However, the current situation is such that in many instances, both options are readily available. Whether you opt for an uncomplicated or a challenging route, you may find it imperative to journey along a path that resonates with your passion for life. Thus, when you eventually leave all else behind and select a path that guides you towards your desired destination, where lifelong contentment awaits, you have made one of the most profound decisions on your journey, fully aware that you have considered both alternatives.

If you ever reflect upon your past, you may wonder about the potential of a world lived to its fullest, guided by your deep self-awareness, where you don't ignore any part of yourself. As we are drawn into a present where yesterday holds no significance, we are challenged to appreciate our lives fully. Art, in essence, is an integral part of life's cycle. Regardless of how dire a situation might have seemed, the solution should ideally align with your true desires within this existence. This underscores the importance of wholehearted dedication to what genuinely brings us happiness.

What might you be missing out on, something that meant a lot for you to thrive, but you can never experience again? Those opportunities in your life that were meant to be opened, leading you towards your ultimate destiny. The journey that was supposed to help you become a more complete version of yourself, which you're leaving behind, and you'll never discover the potential you could have reached. All those anxieties, the things that you fear most in your life, were meant to be conquered to help you grow into a better person. The positive changes that opening those doors would have brought into your life, and now you'll remain trapped in that cage indefinitely.

Who you are right now is unique, and you won't be exactly the same again. This is because you haven't pursued your deepest desires in life, which is crucial for reaching your full potential. When we live in alignment with our passions and dreams, we move forward without looking back, embarking on a path that leads us into the endless future. This journey sometimes diverges, with one path choosing simplicity while the other embraces complexity. However, the simpler path ultimately comes to an end when we pass away, and a farewell ritual is performed, reminding us that we all return to dust and ashes. On the other hand, if you've chosen to be a star by pursuing your dreams, you'll return to the cosmos and shine forever.

It is a common desire for all of us to aspire to become stars. However, life often presents challenges that require patience and a deep understanding. This is the point at which we may feel deprived of the ability to achieve our aspirations. In our lives, we have gained knowledge and learned how to distinguish ourselves through the utilization of our intellectual capabilities. As a result, we will continually be motivated to uncover something distinct and unique in everything we encounter.

The path to abundance and complete fulfillment, that's what we might have named it, becomes attainable when you actively search for meaning in various life circumstances. You embark on a journey of self-discovery, persistently exploring until you uncover that distinct individual residing within you. This is the version of you that holds a profound understanding of every aspect of the universe's creation.

As you grow, you become stronger, your knowledge shines brightly, and you gain confidence in your own perspective. However, there might be moments when you feel a bit envious of those who follow others' ways of thinking, finding their path in life through different viewpoints. But it's important to remember that people have their reasons, and life is about making the most of your experiences. Many have succeeded in this and discovered valuable lessons in places you didn't consider worthwhile. Embracing your unique way of thinking is essential, and you should embrace all aspects of yourself, nurturing your true self from every experience to become the person you truly know you are.

You have great confidence in yourself, even when faced with challenging situations. You are determined not to return to your past self. Now, everyone will need to acknowledge the person you've transformed into, and they won't remember your previous self. You will emerge stronger. You will navigate through life's various experiences, ultimately arriving at the point of your rebirth today. This journey is propelled by the world that has become your new life, a path you comprehend with your own unique abilities.

During challenging times, when you're facing difficulties and witnessing others around you living better lives, you might find yourself wondering, "Why is it me and not someone else?" The reason is that you are important in the grand scheme of life and the future world that will emerge. You don't want to passively observe the universe creating itself while you remain uninvolved. Instead, you aspire to contribute to the creation of a better existence. You live with a strong desire to make your actions meaningful, so that you will be remembered for something truly valuable. This raises questions about the significance of fame and what you can gain from it, as well as the deeper meaning it holds in our lives. What does it truly mean to be famous, and what can fame bring into your life?

When you've found an opportunity to create a lasting legacy that encompasses the essence of life itself, and every aspect of it holds significance, you aspire to become an invaluable asset to the entire world. You are determined not to miss out on the chance to find joy. You've selected a path that revolves around garnering genuine attention, and it constitutes your entire reason for being. You exist for a higher purpose, opting to stand not only for yourself but also to symbolize your spiritual connection with others.

You are a reflection of everyone you hold dear, and your presence extends beyond physical proximity in your daily life. You embody more than just an individual in this world; you personify caring. For those who truly know you and stand alongside you, your voice resonates on their behalf like no one else's. You reject the idea of living within constraints and compromising the quality of life you've witnessed. Your purpose transcends the comprehension of many; you enthusiastically aspire to display your talents.

When your entire focus is on self-improvement, starting from a point of nothingness, you won't return to your former self. Instead, you'll grow, and your existence will endure indefinitely. It's when you recognize your inherent worth and hold that unique aspect of your whole self dear. You acquire the ability to bring joy and enthusiasm to those seeking happiness, and you become skilled at both instructing and inspiring others.

You take care of yourself and strive for perfection by using your life experiences. Some people might not notice all the challenges you faced as you moved from imperfection to excellence. There isn't a daily judge, but you're driven to attain perfection and you change as a result. You understand that it resides within you, and you cultivate it with patience and intelligence until it becomes a part of everyone, regardless of whether it's easy or tough. You persist until you break free from that limiting mindset.

No matter how you felt about the results when you tried to comprehend things your own way, you never gave up until they all became a part of something undeniably beautiful. You carry the beauty in your heart, and you desire everyone to be aware of and witness the precious treasure you possess as a part of life. You've made a conscious decision to engage in a broader realm of knowledge and comprehension, thus participating in a grander sphere of intellect and insight.

When you reflect upon your journey, realizing that you weren't born in your current state, you may wonder who can impede your progress or hinder your path. You hail from a realm of simplicity, where your life was ordinary in every facet. However, you've managed to transform yourself, evolving into a fresh and distinct individual. It is within this newfound self that you've unearthed the essence of life.

You have transformed into someone unique. You made a choice to lead a life among many challenges, a life that wouldn't be straightforward. You left behind simplicity to embrace complexity and sophistication. You've successfully solved the puzzle of your own existence, displaying exceptional qualities as a person. You truly shine, and this isn't just about achieving fame and wealth; it's about living a life filled with quality and meaning.

On a journey that wasn't easy to navigate, you witnessed everything falling into place. There were moments when you were your own worst adversary, obstructing your path to success, yet you persevered and overcame those obstacles. Even in the face of numerous hardships, you never gave up or questioned, 'Why me?' Who can possibly impede your progress? Who can dare deny you the fulfillment of your innermost desires?

Preface

Fame is a quality that we can attain when we strive to improve ourselves. It's not only about becoming well-known for your skills and talents. Sometimes, we find ourselves immersed in our own actions and thoughts, some of which are apparent to others, while others remain hidden. However, as time passes, these actions become evident, and you may find yourself in unexpected situations without realizing it. This sense of wonder can lead you to search everywhere for answers about who you are, but you might struggle to find a solution.

At a certain moment, you come to realize that a vital portion of your existence is devoted to all the knowledge and skills you possess. This realization dawns upon you that true happiness hinges on this very facet of your life. In a peculiar manner, you sense an innate wellspring of inner fortitude and inspiration that can empower you to transcend your past self and become a more deserving and fulfilled individual. You might find yourself embarking on a quest for a path or resolution to an enigmatic dilemma that eludes your understanding and seems perpetually elusive.

Sometimes, in life, you might face a challenging situation or a setback where finding a solution seems impossible. However, if you manage to overcome these obstacles and attain fame, it can transform you into a completely different individual. Often, we find ourselves constrained by our own self-esteem and haunted by our past mistakes, making it difficult to break free from these limitations. While some may attempt to achieve a breakthrough in a moment of inspiration, it is essential to understand that accomplishing this is far from straightforward.

There are various phases in life when you might find yourself feeling stuck, as if you're deep within your own thoughts, and you may want to try everything in your power to attain what you truly deserve to become. However, you might notice that a small part of yourself isn't quite where it should be. If you don't fully prepare yourself for the path to your desired destination, you could find yourself going in circles without ever discovering that final piece of your true self. It's crucial to understand that you'll need every aspect of your being to reach your aspirations. Undoubtedly, you must uncover all that you are before fulfilling your innermost desires.

You should embrace life with all the knowledge you possess, as it aligns with our fundamental purpose, and it's essential not to question why these circumstances have chosen us. Recognize that each of us faces unique challenges that demand varied approaches to understanding them. Remember that within us, there are both inner struggles and external adversaries, but we can conquer them through our dedication. It may begin as a modest notion, yet it can ultimately become the solution to the challenges we encounter due to the mistakes we may make. Achieving this necessitates the unity of our inner selves.

You can learn how to navigate certain things in life, while with others, it's uncertain how to overcome them permanently. You'll need a lot of determination to succeed against all odds. Sometimes, we rely on our knowledge to get through challenging situations. It's remarkable how something you initially do for fun can later become essential for survival. Various situations and circumstances will always shape your identity, and you should aim to become more than just someone people know.

After all the hard work and dedication you've put into everything you know, achieving success becomes crucial for your peace of mind. Sometimes, there might be something even greater waiting for you, and you must continuously invest yourself in it until it becomes the defining aspect of your life. Ultimately, this pursuit defines your path and requires you to make decisive choices about who you've become. Your journey shouldn't be dictated by the opinions of the majority; it should reflect your unique thoughts and values. You won't fully understand what you might lose along the way until you're faced with the challenges that come your way, but that's the nature of life's encounters.

You should aim for a goal that becomes your primary identity in the world, making you independent of everything else that usually represents you. Ensure that you're recognized for your passion and dedication to life, known primarily for that. It's clear that at the start of our lives, we commit ourselves to something, but that commitment should not be half-hearted; you should wholeheartedly embrace your true self.

You have to give a lot, and this is what defeats the enemy within you and brings honor to your entire self. It comes from deep within and allows you to truly live as a human being, leading your own life. So, don't hesitate to give your all until you've reached a full understanding.

You can pursue your goals, whether they are simple or challenging. You can ask yourself thought-provoking questions that are tailor-made for your personal growth journey, helping you become what you truly desire. Life tends to provide us with what we genuinely require. The path to your dreams will always be open, and this is the wonderful aspect of creation. Keep in mind that people may evaluate you based on your knowledge, both what you know and what you may not yet know.

You have the power to recognize when you've gone above and beyond the call of duty in your pursuit of success. This reflects greatly on your character, as it's through such efforts that we forge a lasting legacy. Never question, 'Why me?' Rather, embrace the person you've become through the challenges you've faced. This path is essential to reaching your destination. Without it, you might remain in obscurity indefinitely. To dispel the darkness, you must wholeheartedly devote yourself, giving life a renewed sense of purpose.

Acknowledgements

I want to express my heartfelt gratitude to my beloved wife, who has been an unwavering source of support and strength throughout the entire process of writing and publishing this book. Her constant encouragement and assistance have truly been invaluable, and I am deeply thankful for her unwavering commitment.

I extend my sincere appreciation and thanks to my cherished darling for her tireless dedication and unwavering belief in me as I embarked on this writing journey.

Fame

We all have various motivations for our work, but there comes a moment when you realize that, even though you want to explain why you do what you do, you're also influenced by the same factors that affect everyone else. You may aspire to increase your wealth and yearn for recognition, much like the people we encounter every day. Perhaps you simply wish to pursue your goals in a gracious manner, allowing yourself to stand out as a unique individual driven by a distinct set of principles.

Most people share a common trait deep within themselves. They desire the things that hold significant value for everyone. However, a challenge arises when one needs to determine if they are willing to go to great lengths to attain their desires, regardless of the potential sacrifices required for success. You may have your unique approach to accomplishing your goals, but the additional effort and perseverance expended in the pursuit of these objectives often stem from a shared desire for acknowledgment and recognition. We all yearn for our dedication and strenuous efforts to be acknowledged and celebrated.

It's an irresistible urge that captures people from all walks of life, regardless of their background or motivations, whether it's for the allure of wealth or the allure of fame. We all desire recognition and visibility among the masses, fulfilling a deep-seated need to reach a point where our actions and accomplishments become topics of conversation. We yearn for the day when our deeds are celebrated, making a positive impact on countless lives, even though we acknowledge that this ascent to the pinnacle won't occur overnight. Nevertheless, ascending to the summit remains our primary objective.

Sometimes, it's not just about being known by others, but rather, what you wish to be acknowledged for. We often have clear objectives we aim to accomplish, yet occasionally, we become impatient and desire things prematurely. While we all understand our identities and responsibilities, and we don't necessarily mind gaining recognition for various achievements. It's a common occurrence in the journey of life to feel envious of those who are famous for various reasons. Nevertheless, the key question is, can you remain committed to your goals and become known for your true self and your actions, embracing the authentic individuals we are?

You might not necessarily be a famous actor or a well-known media personality; instead, you might be an inventive individual who has devised your unique methods for accomplishing tasks. You may have no qualms about gaining recognition for your ingenuity. Nevertheless, there are moments when we fail to perceive the perspectives through which the world can introduce us to the broader human population. How can you ascend to such a significant stage in life, or transcend the ordinary elements of reality, in order to gain acknowledgment for your complete self and your life achievements?

Deep within your inner self, you understand that achieving even a modest degree of recognition is truly something to cherish. It would speak volumes about your character and abilities. Conversely, in today's specialized age, it's imperative for each person to have a clear sense of their pursuits. If you view the world from this perspective, witnessing your aspirations materialize won't catch you off guard. As you reach the conclusion, reflect on how you can transcend all obstacles that have held you back and remain dedicated to becoming precisely the person you are meant to be and fulfilling your essential needs.

At some point in your life, you might reach a stage where you've become highly skilled at what you do. However, despite your expertise, you might still sense that the world is limiting your progress and keeping many opportunities hidden from you. It's as though you frequently find yourself trapped in challenging and obscure circumstances. Deep down, it would be more satisfying if you were at least acknowledged for all your talents and abilities. How can you find contentment in this situation? How can you unlock the door to reach a higher level where things happen as they should and where you can perform tasks in the intended manner?

Have you ever wondered how life really shapes us into the individuals we aspire to be or, conversely, the individuals we'd rather avoid becoming? What truly makes us the central figures in the story of our own lives, with a unique and crucial role in history? The answer lies in the intricate workings of our journey, revealing much about our ambitions and the people we strive to become.

Fame can be a wonderful aspect of what we do, especially when compared to everything else. However, it's crucial not to lose sight of your true self and the reasons you became the person you are today. Always keep in mind that reaching fame might require you to act differently from others at times, but reality will always ground you in your true identity. Do you know why you're out there seeking life's experiences? It's because you have responsibilities that extend far beyond merely being in the spotlight.

You will always have to bear these duties alongside you, not only for those you motivate but also because the entire world is watching you, anticipating much from you. People are curious about your perspective on life, and there are high expectations for any influential individual. Your responsibility extends beyond your followers; it pertains to inspiring all of humanity. Many individuals are seeking to discover themselves through your insights, and if you were to inadvertently mislead some of them, they would feel deeply let down.

You are an inspiration not only to children but also to the younger generation, who represent the future of our world. They will bear the responsibility for our universe when you are no longer actively serving humanity. These young individuals are the ones in whom creation has placed its trust. Leading a public life is indeed a wonderful endeavor, but it does come with its fair share of responsibilities. However, you need not alter your essence due to the demands of your public life. The path to achieving happiness and greatness can often be challenging and complex, requiring significant effort and understanding of what it takes to reach that pinnacle.

Deep within, it's hard to go wrong when you're passionate about your actions. What truly transforms your perspective and emotions toward the world is the process of creating concepts, based on everything you've learned. However, numerous challenges may stand in your way as you strive for the freedom to pursue your greatest passion. This is especially true when, in certain instances, or perhaps consistently, it becomes crucial to carry out essential tasks. This shift can undoubtedly reshape your understanding and emotional connection to various aspects of life. To achieve this, persistence is key, as you're determined not to compromise on your goals. You're determined to follow your life's chosen path, having recognized the significance of your actions.

Who has the power to alter your knowledge or actions if they align with the truth or correctness of your understanding? The answer is no one. Where do you place your trust, and upon what do you rely to ensure the certainty of your actions? Does it rest upon a particular entity over which you wish to exert control, yet find it beyond your grasp? Are you self-sufficient in all your endeavors, possessing all the necessary qualities, or do you require assistance from others? The introduction of external influences may lead to confusion. However, if you only need yourself, then you cannot go astray. Therefore, if you ever find yourself lost, it may signify errors in many of your initial actions.

Sometimes, no matter who you are, there comes a moment when you simply require someone's assistance to comprehend your current situation – someone who can provide solace and reassurance. Consequently, if you find yourself without such a companion, it can become quite challenging when things take a turn for the worse. On occasion, it's difficult to discern the source of inaccuracy, and these circumstances possess the power to transform you, guiding you towards an unfamiliar path in life. A single individual can perform an action with expectations of a grander outcome, only to furnish you with an identity that deviates significantly from your true self, thus effecting profound change within you.

You may find it challenging to deal with things that are unfamiliar to you. The only thing people truly know and understand well is themselves. Becoming involved in something outside of your comfort zone typically happens when you become exhausted and decide to let go of your true self. At that point, you may be more open to embracing whatever opportunities come your way. This is how you can become a part of something that may seem irrelevant to you, and it might be difficult for you to find harmony with it.

Sometimes, there comes a time when you can't be yourself, and someone else steps in to take your role or simply be like you. You might wonder why this happens. Is it because you're not meeting your goals, or is it because you've lost the motivation to continue? Often, all it takes is persistent and dedicated effort to keep moving forward, even when you're unsure of the outcome. It's better to complete the journey than to leave the work unfinished.

How do you reconcile not reaching all the things you've always wanted throughout your entire life, having to exist without ever accomplishing that goal? How can you find inner harmony with the person you've become, how can you come to terms with yourself after enduring numerous challenges, and finally deciding to relinquish your true self, your greatest aspiration, and everything of significance to you? Certainly, you can't comprehend every aspect of life and how all the pieces fit together, but you shouldn't label yourself as inept. The journey isn't solely about seizing opportunities; it's about establishing your identity as a brand, a feat you've managed to achieve despite facing formidable obstacles.

You don't need to feel jealous of others as you journey through life. It's important to stay true to yourself and not compare your life to someone else's, wishing you were in their shoes. As you venture out into the world, remember this: aim to become the best version of yourself, and don't let external situations or circumstances change who you are. You'll discover ways to make sense of things, so it's essential to maintain your authenticity. Focus on achieving success in your unique way, even though there may be moments when you consider adapting to something different. Deep down, you know that's not your true self.

What have you decided to embrace as your identity that proves challenging to bear, evolving into a weight you find increasingly burdensome? Is it the collective demands of society, the diverse ways of people, and their myriad viewpoints? Such a multitude of factors can accumulate, making your journey seem arduous. Despite progressing forward, something seems to persistently impede your path, and internally, you sense an urge for transformation. However, remember that there is no necessity to dwell on the past.

Continue to live your life, and perhaps you may find yourself pondering how to endure the challenges it presents. After all, your happiness is deeply connected to the journey you've chosen for yourself. This path can offer us valuable lessons, explaining why it's important to persevere even when faced with daunting obstacles. Never lose faith in your new life; instead, explore alternative ways to meet your immediate needs, all in pursuit of bringing your ideas to fruition.

This is what could make life more manageable in the long run. Even though today may be difficult, the things you're thinking of quitting or losing hope in could turn out to be much more valuable tomorrow. The very next day, they might become a source of great strength for you. So, if you ever feel like giving up, think about what your future might be like down the road. Consider what alternatives you might encounter on your journey to success. Remember that many things in life require time and effort before you see the desired results.

It might seem like achieving this goal isn't easy at all. It requires constant focus and effort. You can't reach it overnight. It might appear impossible, but the only option you should give yourself is to work towards becoming exactly what you've chosen to be. Don't worry about how or when it will happen. All you need to know is that you should start.

You don't need to worry about knowing every detail of how things will happen. What's important is that you've done your part and followed the necessary steps. But how can you stay confident when you're uncertain about the future? Just believe in the idea that inspired you in the first place. That's all you need to reach your destination.

Even though it may not have occurred as you initially expected, it turned out to be one of the most significant accomplishments you've ever experienced. Who could have foreseen that something that originated from nothing would eventually become an integral part of the most influential or thrilling creation ever? This fact speaks volumes about your character. Perhaps you could have gained extensive knowledge about life and the world around you but still remained unchanged, preserving your core identity without altering a single aspect of yourself.

We discover many things about our goals and dreams as we journey through life. We also learn how to turn these aspirations into reality. To achieve a strong sense of self-worth, it's important to be recognized and acknowledged for your talents and abilities. Embrace your ideas as they are and don't try to be someone you're not; you're a unique individual. Uphold the honesty and reputation of your personal brand, and the extent of your success depends on how broad you wish to expand your horizons. The world offers endless opportunities for you to explore and make your own.

As a person who wants to understand things better, there's nothing hidden from you. You have the ability to be anything you want, but it's important to carefully choose your path. Many opportunities are available, and it doesn't matter which path you choose, you'll gain the necessary knowledge as you progress towards your goal.

People enjoy celebrating the birth of excellent ideas. When your concept succeeds, you may attract many people interested in representing your brand. They can come in various forms and from different directions to showcase your identity. This aspect of the life you've chosen is important to grasp. These individuals will assist in performing specific functions that you cannot accomplish independently.

You should not deprive yourself of anything essential to your being. However, it's crucial to avoid allowing it to dominate your choices when striving to fulfill your destiny. Keep in mind that your primary goal isn't solely to accumulate wealth. Rather, you aspire to gain recognition for your positive contributions to humanity. Your aim is to be recognized and appreciated for your true self and your meaningful actions.

Achieving all your desires doesn't happen instantly; it takes time and effort. If you push yourself too much, it might seem like you're trying to exploit the situation. Many challenges require a significant amount of perseverance, whether or not you consider yourself an intelligent individual. You may also need to exert considerable effort because gaining a deep understanding of things hinges on your unwavering determination. Once you successfully accomplish your goals, you won't have any reason to dwell on the past.

Now that you've set a new goal for yourself to achieve, or a milestone to reach, it all hinges on your journey towards greater knowledge and surpassing the boundaries of your current understanding. This entails placing a substantial amount of faith in yourself and your endeavors. Our choices about who we aspire to become are always valid. You might encounter obstacles at the outset, but with persistence, you will eventually ascend to a higher plane of existence, where abstract concepts materialize into tangible realities. If you tirelessly dedicate yourself to this pursuit, it will find acceptance among fellow humans and become a well-established aspect of human life.

We all aspire to become better individuals, seeking acceptance and understanding that we're not fundamentally different from others. It's essential to recognize our commonality with everyone. However, when you cultivate a deep passion for a purpose and commit yourself to it with unwavering determination, you have the potential to attain greatness. Persistently work towards aligning your spiritual self with the person you aspire to be. Remember, the path to self-realization is ever-present, and all it requires is a lifelong dedication.

Realize that you've embarked on a fresh stage of self-control, though you'll forever remain the same individual you were before. Yet, in this new chapter, you must constantly strive until your previous existence gradually recedes. You need not hail from the realm of exceptional humans to accomplish something remarkable. It's crucial not to allow your past to dictate your future and the person you aspire to become. Although it may diminish your sense of belonging, recognize that you can embrace normalcy in the path you've chosen. Take charge of your destiny, commit to adhering to the principles of discipline, and transform into a being worthy of admiration.

To succeed in life, you must honor your commitments and strive to meet the expectations set for you, no matter the sacrifices required. Avoid letting down not only yourself but also those who have faith in your abilities. Aim to become the person you were meant to be: someone with great self-discipline, unwavering focus, and deep respect for others. Cultivate the skill of harmonious interaction with everyone you encounter.

Life used to be simple and ordinary, but it has transformed significantly due to your desires. Now, you bear additional duties that accompany you daily. How much did your desires truly matter to you? Because unexpected events can unfold, it's crucial to understand how your current life unfolded. If your prayers have been answered, take joy in the fact that you didn't struggle to fit into every situation or face rejection and hopelessness without any alternatives.

In life, there's a level playing field where no one gets special treatment. People attain their positions based on their knowledge and skills, and you won't notice this if you're not putting in effort. What you really need is to be certain that your actions are correct. It's crucial to grasp the concepts thoroughly because it's not a privilege; it's something you must earnestly strive for. You need to work diligently, day and night, to succeed.

It's important to understand that achieving your dreams is possible for anyone, regardless of their background. You have the potential to make a name for yourself and share your unique story with the world. Embrace your true self, and it can become a reality if you truly love what you do and carry a deep passion within you, extending your influence to touch the lives of many.

Even when you face challenges along the way, never give up hope. You have a strong desire to achieve many things in life, so keep that passion deep within your heart. Don't act like you're on a noble mission; you are fully conscious that your way of doing things can influence people. Your goal is to introduce people to something that will transform their behavior, and yet inside, you sense that you are enduring significant trials.

In simple terms, if you know what you're doing, make sure you do it in a way that makes it clear to everyone what you mean and what your exact intentions are. If you ever feel confused or uncertain along the way, always remind yourself of the main reason behind everything you're doing. Your ultimate goal is to make things better, and this should be something you always keep in mind at every stage of your life. Your top priority should always be to help people heal and understand themselves.

A strong foundation represents your sincere desire to make a positive impact on the lives of others. When you offer something in return for who you are, you can't make a mistake. If you hold this core value in your heart, you can start from a humble beginning and grow over time. While youth may sometimes lead you through uncertain and challenging times, as you progress, the passage of time will prove the value of your actions and your vision for how things should be accomplished. Everything you seek in life lies along this path.

If you're uncertain about how to show genuine love and compassion towards fellow human beings, you may find yourself feeling lost. It's essential to cultivate a love that protects your relationships and ensures you play a meaningful role in others' lives. Your actions can either offer healing or cause harm to someone. Seek a sense of acceptance, where your understanding of life is acknowledged and embraced, becoming a beacon of hope for the future.

Life has changed, and new responsibilities have found their way to you. It's important to treat everyone with respect and kindness. Keep in mind that you had many options in life, but you decided to face and overcome various challenges on your journey to becoming who you are today, following your deepest desires.

In life, it's important to stay open to the many experiences it offers. You'll encounter a lot of opportunities to learn and grow. Amidst it all, remember to hold onto your true self, your core values. These are the qualities that define who you are and will remain with you in the long run. While fame may come your way, don't compromise your principles to achieve it. Be aware that challenges may arise, tests that could potentially alter your character or even endanger your existence. These trials might tempt you to change and become someone you're not, unless you possess the resilience needed to stay true to your authentic desires and purpose in life.

You might never have had the opportunity to gain knowledge beyond the life you've wholeheartedly dedicated yourself to. Sometimes, when individuals gaze into your eyes, comprehending your true desires within the context of your own existence can prove challenging. Yet, there is a significant element that holds immense importance; it's the very objective you've tirelessly striven to achieve. By virtue of love and unwavering commitment, you gain insight into your past failures, alongside the possibility of others attempting to emulate your journey. These circumstances stand as trials within the journey of life, pushing you to your limits until you can no longer endure.

Understand that reality often presents challenges in life, and you can observe this when you engage in any form of creativity. Every endeavor worth pursuing is bound to test your abilities. Instead of resenting these challenges, embrace them, for they are an integral part of the path leading to your desires. Many obstacles that block your way might have arisen elsewhere. In a short span, you may encounter formidable difficulties that seem insurmountable. Yet, if you manage to thrive under such conditions, nothing can hold you back or diminish your passion for creativity.

You may have faced situations that were exceptionally demanding and profoundly stressful, making productivity seem impossible. However, through patience and perseverance, you managed to overcome these obstacles. While they may have altered your experiences, don't let them change your core self or rob you of your love for life. Remember, when the time comes to make your mark, let your creativity shine, standing out as something unique and unprecedented.

The blessings you possess can fade away, and as a person, you can become so fragile that you might even undermine your main life goals. But this is just the way life unfolds. Such experiences can have a profound impact on your perspective and how you respond to life. Deep down, you recognize that you weren't meant to alter your essence, yet you may find yourself sitting there, filled with remorse for the person you've become.

Have you ever wondered why life often feels like an arduous journey, full of obstacles? Sometimes, if you want to make the world a better place or improve a situation, it's best to look elsewhere. When everything else vanishes, what remains is the essence of life within you. So, don't allow those obstacles to consume you; if your aim is to bring about change in society, persist in your pursuit.

In those very moments when you feel challenged, there's much to learn about yourself. Don't wage battles against everything that blocks your path, for some challenges are meant to assist you in achieving your life objectives. Anything that insists on rendering situations insurmountable, thereby impeding your progress, can become your life's adversary. Regardless of the outcome of the struggles you face in discovering your true self, refrain from transforming yourself and your life into adversaries of all that life offers. If it's a battle out there, fight to make the world a better place.

Chapter One

Crown by love

No matter what journey you've been on or the battles you've faced inside, it might seem like the pain inside you can never be healed. You could be anyone, hailing from a place only you truly understand because of what you've been through. Finding a way to recover from those experiences becomes a unique path that one must navigate alone. It often feels like the things we've lost cannot be replaced, and our hearts can shatter when pursuing our deepest desires. Although you may eventually reach your destination, the struggle to make sense of a world that doesn't align with our expectations can persist for a considerable time, making it challenging for our lives to find stability.

There are many ways to approach life, but one path that can lead you to a point where success seems irrelevant is a life without genuine love. We possess so much from the world we come from, but if you've never experienced happiness, what are you clinging to? Fond memories serve as anchors to our past selves; without them, we often grasp onto things that no longer define who we are.

You might have endured the pain of troubled relationships due to your actions, but it's essential to have someone who can guide you towards correction or offer acceptance. Without that support, there may be little reason to continue living in the same manner. One bewildering aspect is not knowing how to navigate life when love disappears, causing you to dwell in the past.

You should search for an idea that matches your personality and aligns with your goals and aspirations. This idea should be something you are extremely familiar with and have a strong belief in its potential for success. Cling to this idea with the knowledge that it holds the promise of happiness. It's essential to understand that only genuine love can propel you toward your desired destination. No matter how challenging the journey may become due to unfavorable circumstances, maintain your course in the direction of love. Changing yourself or your life significantly may seem tempting, but our core identity is shaped by the commitments we make. You should resist the urge to transform into someone else for the sake of pleasing others. It's vital to stay true to yourself, as your existence has a unique purpose that can bring meaning to others' lives.

Realizing this truth marks a transformative stage in our journey. From there, we can move forward in a new direction. We cannot make up for the misunderstandings and lost time in our past, especially when we avoid addressing unresolved issues in our relationships. Some people may seek solace in alternative pursuits like careers, allowing love to slip through their grasp. This can lead to lingering feelings of dissatisfaction. It often feels like we live in a world designed to torment us, forcing us into roles that are not a natural fit for our true selves.

Many of the challenges we face in life are not normal or easy to endure. They can be suffocating and drain our energy. While suffering may persist, there is little room for genuine love in such a world. Our true essence is eroded, leaving us with little of our original selves. Perhaps this occurs because we chase after worldly desires that are not aligned with our innate blessings.

True love has always been elusive, and as we embark on unfamiliar paths, we may encounter even greater difficulties. Love can sometimes falter prematurely. Perhaps life intended for us to remain true to our original selves, staying in the blessings we were born with, rather than pursuing endless worldly desires. Our true heritage is divine, yet we often curse ourselves by coveting too much from this world.

The more you desire money, or the more eager you are to become famous, the more likely it is that you'll find yourself living a normal life, constrained by societal norms and expectations. The farther you aspire to travel on the path to fame, the stronger the opposition you'll encounter from those who dislike you. You may have noticed this because life rarely offers easy solutions.

When you wake up with a burning desire for fame, it can feel as if everything is falling apart, and you may believe you can fix it, but it's not that simple. While it may seem that some people around us effortlessly achieve their dreams, such instances are rare. It's as if, in the ordinary world, there's no clear place for what we aspire to be, and we often feel envious before gaining a clear perspective on the world. You might wish to make a significant impact and hope the world will change when it embraces you, but it could remain largely unchanged.

The tales you hear about love and fame are not mere stories; they reflect the reality of that level of existence. Perhaps we've sacrificed love for individualism, thinking that money would come our way anyway. But there must be something more to it than riches because if you become obsessed with fame, you're drawn in by an addictive force.

Is it that everything related to true love and happiness should never be postponed? We crave these emotions so intensely in the present that denying ourselves such feelings seems impossible. Imagine going through a day without them; it would feel like disconnection from everything that makes us human, as if we're no longer part of life. We hear about people in love and how they share such profound emotions.

Money often appears to be the primary source of problems, but pursuing fame can lead to a curse even in unexpected places where you shouldn't have met your demise. Where has the tenderness of the heart disappeared to? It seems like we can no longer be a part of it. Everything has become a relic of the past, and we search for it, even though it's rarely found in its true form again.

When genuine love isn't valued, the source of money becomes insignificant. Despite our continuous efforts in various pursuits, our ultimate goal is to understand how to secure our rightful portion in life. This quest for something meaningful persists throughout our existence. As long as we remain human, the desire to achieve something remains our primary purpose. Amid all the experiences we've encountered, love stands apart. It is a constant presence, a birthright intended to accompany us throughout our journey.

However, if you choose to dedicate your life to achieving recognition or gaining fame among unfamiliar faces, you may notice that relationships tend to falter. What erodes the power of love and the capacity to be embraced? Determining when you've invested enough to regain it becomes an enigma.

Our aspirations to evolve are numerous, yet we shouldn't lose sight of the present. Could the love we've lost have been diverted elsewhere? Do we need to channel more effort into nurturing our relationships? Perhaps, true love requires active involvement. Although one cannot change their essence, redirecting the desire for fame and fortune towards life might entail a strenuous endeavor to reconnect with our innate selves.

Considering that we are inherently designed to love, it seems elusive to attain the level of global recognition and life satisfaction without sacrificing a part of our authentic selves. Our genetic makeup predisposes us to form connections, coursing through our veins, yearning for a fulfilling relationship. Sadly, the pursuit of true love has become increasingly rare due to the transformations we undergo.

You may realize that your enthusiasm for fame has caused you to forfeit love long before achieving it. You've journeyed too deeply alone, far more than necessary, making it challenging to envision a committed relationship. You might even doubt whether you can recover this lost essence, pondering how to heal from this predicament.

Sometimes, we find ourselves caught between two worlds, trapped by our own desires. We yearn to be known for something greater than what we are now. Regardless of the challenges we face on our journey, our hearts compel us to keep moving forward. In these moments, we may become lost, spending countless nights alone, and we begin to recognize the importance of someone's presence. This lesson often emerges from the emptiness we feel along the way.

Perhaps there are different types of love: one that is natural and another that is modern. "Natural love" occurs when someone accepts us as we are, without any effort. Imagine someone freely giving themselves to you because they believe you deserve love, without any need for you to please them. They are simply there for you, and you start to wonder what can disrupt this natural tenderness towards life. Despite the world's advancements and changes in various aspects, we remain steadfast in preserving our true selves in our relationships.

What truly holds the power to unravel the love we once shared, regardless of our evolution? This love embraced all that we were, and now, it seems we are no longer deserving of such a precious gift that once cared about us. We are left to seek our own understanding to find a worthy relationship. How can something so sacred be entrusted to our own will and abilities?

How can you determine if someone is the right person for you? Can you ever truly comprehend all the factors that contribute to a deep connection? True love, which was once freely given, now appears to come at a steep price. You may attempt to purchase it, but there is no price that can make someone's heart pour itself out to you.

The world we aspired to conquer often proves to be harsh and unforgiving. You may have devoted your entire self to something you love, expecting the world to embrace you with open arms. Yet, for the first time, you find that circumstances have turned against you, and love has left you with a shattered heart. Unlike the world where true love was freely given before you even sought it, now it seems elusive.

In this newfound level of understanding, we must first succeed in all our life pursuits before we can experience happiness. Love was once lost to us, and if we ever find it, it should be the crowning achievement of our efforts. Whether we are aware of it or not, can we hold onto it, or will we let it slip away? We must fully realize that our current possessions do not necessarily bring us happiness. We can't resist a rare opportunity to be free, as it is these relationships that set us free.

We often surround ourselves with things that no longer serve us, diverting our focus and spending too much time without considering that we could have utilized that time more wisely. Now, we might believe that these possessions can offer us something valuable in return, and we continue to hold onto them, not realizing that our time could have been better spent on more deserving pursuits.

Although it's challenging to break away from the common way of life that defines our reality, is it truly worth it to turn away from the expectations of others and become who we are meant to be? Spending time with people who no longer align with our current selves doesn't yield any benefits; in fact, we lose more of ourselves than we gain.

The situation worsens when we insist on pursuing something that no longer aligns with our true selves. We dedicate our efforts to an aspect of life where we are no longer accepted, and the standard of living we adhere to no longer reflects our worth or our true aspirations. Is it worth holding onto, knowing that our minds can never find peace because we don't belong there?

We should surrender ourselves to the pursuit of our true desires, even when we know our minds no longer belong in that old place. True love exists where we are deserving of all that we have dedicated ourselves to, including the life we choose to embrace. In the realm of true love, we are cherished for everything that we are, and none of our qualities go to waste; we are valued throughout our lives.

Do you ever feel like you want a different kind of life, even if nobody you know wants the same thing? It's like you're on a journey towards a life that's unique to you. But sometimes, you end up in situations where you don't know how to escape, and you wonder, how far is it from where you are now to where you want to be? Is the gap so vast that you're lost in the middle of it all? Somewhere deep inside, there must be a path that's so convincing that turning back isn't an option.

You might find that you're not fully comfortable with everything life throws at you, especially when it comes to love and the desire for fame. It's not that you're struggling with a lot; it's more about figuring out which direction to go. Do you let go of the things you could have had in the past and hold onto your dreams? We all wished love were simple so we could be certain about who we want to be, instead of feeling lost when we dive deep into it.

The truth is, you're not there yet, so there's no one who truly understands you. You have to leave behind your past to navigate this uncertain phase of life. It's tough to not have a sense of belonging and to seek balance in whatever is available, even when there's not much. You find yourself standing alone, relying on your knowledge.

Is it necessary to be alone on this journey, or is it normal to keep moving forward like this? Did we face all the usual life battles from the moment we were born, and now we're encountering new challenges that reflect who we truly are, challenges that offer more than the world we come from?

As you journey toward the stars, you engage in new struggles in the pursuit of the world where you wish to be reborn. Part of this endeavor necessitates solitude. You must fully embrace your envisioned self until it becomes your essence. You must shape yourself into the person you aspire to be before inviting others into your life. If you lack the necessary strength, you may falter on this path. You must persevere through your battles until you are ultimately reborn into the world you aspire to join.

You must cultivate your growth in this aspect of your life until you attain the worthiness that satisfies your desires. There's a compelling reason why you aspired to become a star. Something about that life intrigued you until you decided to become a part of it. It might be the allure of the lifestyle or the rewards of your efforts. Be honest with yourself; you pursued this path because you believed in yourself, your endeavors, and your deep affection for this life.

Talent is one thing, and a portion of it can be channeled into various pursuits. However, focusing on fame, wealth, or affluence reveals a singular eagerness for this life. Such a focus cannot be rationalized. Your eagerness stems from a desire for something specific, while any other justifications may be mere pretenses. Obstacles stand in your way because this is the nature of the world; it demands much from those who seek its rewards.

It's not always typical for us humans to follow the same familiar path that we've grown accustomed to. Sometimes, you might find yourself standing there, pondering what it takes to break through to the other side. It could mean expanding your knowledge and pushing beyond the limits of your usual efforts, without worrying about failure. Simply believe in your ability to succeed as you move forward. Every endeavor has its rewards, including the love and financial means necessary for the life you desire.

Think back to your upbringing; you didn't start with everything handed to you. When it comes to love, do you give your heart freely, or do you hope to meet someone special along your journey? Are you chasing a dream, hoping to attain the best in life? Do you fall in love easily or wait for your perfect match?

Is striving for what we truly desire diminishing our significance, forcing us to settle for less than we deserve? Not having everything we desire along the way can sometimes discourage us from pursuing our best life. You may contemplate surrendering to anything that comes your way, but deep down, you know that's not who you are. You aspire for something much better than your current circumstances.

In challenging times, we often seek support from people we might not choose if we had everything we needed. When you feel deeply ashamed of who you are, you may give in to various temptations, even though you know you should aim for more. Along the way, we all crave comfort, and some people can't bear solitude. On the other hand, it's essential to practice self-discipline. Loneliness doesn't always result from someone rejecting you; sometimes, it arises due to your life choices.

Regardless of the cause, remember that love can fade when you're not where you should be. Perhaps you've been hurt before, and ever since, you've refused to accept anything less than what you truly desire. You might try seeking solace in others, but it could lead to the same unsatisfying situation.

Certain circumstances can hurt you so deeply that they shatter your world and force you to distance yourself from your previous life. You envision a future as the only place where you can rediscover yourself, a future where you're mending your broken pieces. Life seems distant and unreachable, like a star in the sky. To make that journey, you must first identify the essence of life within you that you need to hold onto.

Life often presents challenges that test our faith and can lead us astray. When you strive to unlock your full potential, it's crucial to resist settling for mediocrity along the journey. This is because settling can hinder your ability to live the life you truly deserve. Additionally, imposing limits on yourself can be a significant setback when you should be spreading your wings and expanding your horizons.

You must reach a point of unwavering determination where you unequivocally desire and demand everything you rightly merit. No one, not even money, should be able to withhold the love and abundance you require. To shine brightly like a star means harboring dreams and pursuing them relentlessly, regardless of the obstacles that may stand in your way. You will discover ingenious ways to overcome challenges, all while remaining steadfast in your pursuit of everything you desire—be it wealth, love, or any other aspiration. Maintaining this unwavering commitment to your core values will inspire and resonate with many hearts, emphasizing the enduring worth of your humanity.

It appears that there is a lot standing in the way of who we are and our aspirations. Our dreams are the most important things in our lives, keeping us going. Imagine your deepest desire vanishing before your very eyes, knowing it's not what you wished for, and now you must accept something you didn't want. Hoping for something good defines us and our futures. You hold onto hope to make sense of it all. Sometimes, many obstacles can hinder your progress, and there's no one to blame for that.

This means you shouldn't base your hopes and desires on someone else's life.

What truly matters is what you can do. We often have no choice but to pursue our ambitions because failing to reach them can deeply hurt your soul. Your dreams may become the only reason you keep going. While you dream and strive to achieve, you might feel devastated when they don't come true.

Dreams can disrupt your life, and it's not fair to blame the world for dashing your hopes. Building your dreams based on someone else's understanding won't work. You must chase your own goals on your own terms. If you fail, it's likely because you're trying to force something that isn't meant to be. So, strive to create your own path toward your desires and work diligently for what you want. Use your own knowledge and understanding to find solutions tailored to your success.

Life can sometimes hold you back so much that you find yourself yearning for a simpler path. You may spend years in this situation, wishing that people could truly understand you. Perhaps you feel that you relied too much on luck to reach your current position, which may involve living under someone else's roof and helping them achieve their dreams. However, your true potential lies in aligning your visions with your knowledge.

When you operate based on your own understanding, pursuing your goals without hesitation, you increase your chances of reaching success or your desired destination. Developing confidence in your knowledge and thought process is essential. If you can't envision a path to your goals without relying on others, your visions lack a solid foundation. It can be challenging to let go of desires that seem unattainable, but having a clear mental picture of your objectives is ultimately more fulfilling.

In the journey toward your aspirations, you'll learn valuable lessons, even if the outcome isn't precisely what you envisioned. There are times when you want everything from life, and you strive diligently to attain it. You may endure pain and hardships along the way, but you can succeed.

Occasionally, we dream big without considering how to turn those dreams into reality. To make these dreams come true, it's crucial to rely on your own understanding. While others may assist you in some aspects, not everything can be achieved through their guidance. Difficulty arises when you lack comprehension about the practical steps required to reach your goals. If you involve others in your plans, it indicates a gap in your knowledge of achieving your objectives.

Creating a solid plan for your goals relies heavily on self-reliance. You become dependable when it concerns matters of love; it's something we discover together. The way we pursue our desires varies greatly, but you should establish a firm foundation, something that won't let you down.

It all begins with your wishes, yet sometimes you're unsure how to achieve them. This can be quite perplexing when you're desperately seeking that missing piece of life's puzzle. Eventually, you may come to terms with the fact that not everything will unfold as you envisioned. You shouldn't torment yourself with unattainable dreams.

Planning and striving for unattainable goals can be tough when you realize you can't reach the heart of humanity and effect significant change. Even if you don't achieve them in a timely manner, it's preferable to be late than to face the harsh truth that not everything unfolds exactly as you wished.

Life is often different from what we expect, and if you can't change the world entirely, it's okay to aim for achievable goals. You may aspire to attain wealth, love, a loving family, and a successful career where you are well-established. However, sometimes these dreams may remain unfulfilled, and you might find yourself continually daydreaming about them.

While everything may seem reasonable, the world might block your path if you lack expertise in certain areas of life. You shouldn't push yourself beyond your limits. In such cases, it's perfectly fine to accept your current situation. Nonetheless, you should strive to maintain your inner spark and not lose hope entirely. Even when faced with challenging circumstances, you can make small sacrifices to lead a fulfilling life, ensuring you have both love and financial stability.

Love should not be an impossible dream, even if it sometimes feels like you're giving too much and getting nothing in return. Love eventually becomes essential in life. Don't give up on the search for it. Fight for it with determination. Money also plays a significant role in one's life, and having a dignified life is essential. While love may be elusive at times, you shouldn't allow it to be absent from your life. Work to create a loving environment and settle for nothing less than genuine love.

Never abandon your pursuit of love. Discover the unique qualities within you, and cherish the person you are. Strive to make love a cornerstone of your life, and let it be the culmination of your efforts. If you have lived life as intended, your endeavors will eventually lead you to true love, and love will embrace you in return.

Chapter Two

The only solution

You commit your full effort and dedication to a specific task or entity until it becomes your sole path forward. Through this, you gain a deep understanding of what is essential for success. This commitment may grow so strong and influential that even if alternative options exist, you no longer consider them. Instead, you persist in your efforts to excel in your chosen endeavor. This leads to self-reflection, as you wonder how you managed to grasp insights from various available avenues for human beings. While this journey could have been strenuous, stressful, and demotivating, you found ways to connect and relate.

As human beings, we encounter various challenges while seeking a purpose to devote our lives to. You may have faced hardships that are hard to forget. However, from these experiences, you have cultivated valuable knowledge that guides you forward, rendering a return to your previous self impossible. Instead, you strive to extract meaning from these life chapters.

Our continuous growth is shaped by the obstacles we encounter. We may become stuck in one place, unable to ignore our struggles. Only from within can we become the solution to the challenges we face, thus improving ourselves and our circumstances.

Sometimes, the struggle lies in finding solutions and dedicating everything we have to our endeavors and our lives, integrating ourselves into the world through our actions. Our lives reflect the faith we hold in our goals, and we persevere to survive these trials. Consequently, our health, wealth, and daily routines become intertwined with our self-discovery.

Even if a path back were available, it would seem meaningless, for it is through the solutions we apply to our daily challenges that our lives acquire purpose. These solutions answer our questions about how we reached this point. Once too weak to cope with life, we have transformed into individuals who can move confidently in the right direction.

When you face a situation you cannot navigate, you begin to realize that much of what you once knew no longer aligns with how you should lead your life. Your current self no longer fits into the reality of your surroundings. There is a limit to what you can endure, and the trials and tribulations begin to impact every aspect of your life.

Every day, we find ourselves in situations that seem impossible to escape from. It's not because we lack faith in ourselves, but rather because we, as human beings, don't possess all-encompassing knowledge. The circumstances we face may have evolved into what they are today, and it's not easy to simply move past them. Sometimes, life pushes us to the breaking point, requiring a significant event to disrupt our routines. You may feel compelled not to give up because you matter to this world and those around you. Quitting would not define you as a failure.

This situation prompts a deep examination of who we've become. Along the way, we must decide if we truly embody the values we profess. There's no justification for not striving to be someone of worth. The question on everyone's mind is: What will you become? Deep within you, there exists untapped potential, and surrendering would erase all that people recognize in you. What would quitting signify? Would it label you as a failure? It's a critical juncture where you have the opportunity to achieve greatness in your life.

So, how do we let go? Do we simply surrender, or do we need to reevaluate our priorities along the way? We've reached a point where one goal takes precedence over others. Instead of following the conventional path, you're now steering towards your ultimate objective. Remember, to become a meaningful individual, you must have a part of your life that holds significance, earning the respect of those around you.

There must be a profound purpose in your life that you're eager to attain, even if it won't come easily. What will you do when you can't have everything you adore about this world? The essence of striving for something vital in our lives lies in satisfying our hunger for our dreams. It's when you set an important goal ahead, one you're fervently determined to achieve. Losing hope in such an objective could lead to lifelong regret.

This objective might be driven by what matters most to you, your ultimate mission. It could revolve around love or the means to attain financial freedom, enabling you to cherish what you value most. Sometimes, our goals differ from the mainstream, and if they come to fruition, they can reshape people's perceptions of us and our endeavors. Often, others may not take our goals seriously. Witnessing someone's dreams become reality can be a surprising revelation. Despite the challenges, have faith in your vision before the world comprehends your actions and their impact on people's lives.

Right now, you might not have concrete evidence to prove your capabilities or the unique path you wish to tread in life. Your accomplishments might appear limited, and you're aware that not many have ventured this way before. Nevertheless, your determination burns brightly, and you crave the trust and faith of others, understanding that this journey is essential to your very existence. People form their opinions, each viewing the world through their own lens.

Once, you were like many, lacking faith in the possible. Through unwavering determination and self-awareness, you discovered that the seemingly insurmountable is not as daunting as it seems. You learned to believe in yourself, recognizing your worth and your potential to make a difference in the world. We all embark on unique journeys towards our vision of life. The question is, what are you willing to do to achieve it? Where does your faith reside? Do you trust that inner voice whispering that nothing is beyond reach?

Much can transpire, but a new beginning and the restoration of normalcy depend on you. Life's renewal starts within us; if your mind isn't aligned, no one can pull you in the right direction. We must rely on ourselves first, breaking free from our limitations to see the true potential. We often overlook opportunities and waste time waiting for miracles. However, true responsibility for your life extends beyond daily routines.

You have the power to pursue what truly matters to you, whether it's self-improvement, education, or leadership. But this requires unwavering determination, and your journey can inspire many. It's crucial to understand why it matters to you.

If you possess the eagerness and accept that there's no turning back, realizing that merely existing won't suffice, it's time to take responsibility for your life. If external forces truly cared for us, the world would be different; there would be no struggles, homelessness, or starvation. Thus, taking charge of our well-being is fundamental to finding happiness in life. We must carefully tend to our needs and not entrust our well-being solely to others.

When you pursue something with all your heart, it's like having a superpower. As humans, we have this incredible ability to follow our deepest desires. Even if you face failures in other areas of life, that one thing you truly want becomes your defining purpose. It makes you an essential person in your own life.

The most crucial aspect is recognizing the reality around you. Those who achieve what they want are often smart, devoted, or strong individuals. Merely having a passion or desire might not be enough. You may need to wake up and be fiercely determined. Regardless of your age, consider both the advantages and disadvantages. Handle them and strive for the breakthrough. We may all be in different places, but life reflects our capabilities.

You can take pride in your efforts, believing you're the best, but beyond your bubble, you must persevere, even when you feel drained. There's no last place; there's only being the best. You may not conquer the world, but you can win somewhere. It could be within the confines of your innermost desires. Break free from those constraints and stand out in your chosen field.

It may seem like a daunting task, and you may not always know the right way, but give it your all. Remember that one opportunity can change your life. Pour your genuine self into it so that even when you achieve your dream, you can't recall how you did it. It's about dedicating your life and efforts every day until, almost miraculously, it all falls into place. And before you know it, you've achieved something beyond comprehension by many.

The most important part of what we do is setting ourselves free. Holding yourself back by not fully committing to your goals can be a hindrance. Taking that small step, showing dedication to your tasks, liberates your whole self. When you wake up, you'll find that you've transformed. This journey may seem challenging, but true devotion can break through even the toughest obstacles, and all you need is unwavering dedication.

What's truly incredible about personal endeavors is that every effort counts. You have the freedom to pursue your desires at your own pace, whether you have the capacity for a lot or a little. There's no one holding you back; it's all about you. So, when you learn to put in the necessary effort, your work starts to make sense, because it must make sense and reach a level of excellence. While we may come from different backgrounds, we all share the potential to achieve something remarkable in our lives, and the key always lies within our grasp, believing in our ability to reach our highest potential.

If you don't believe in yourself, you won't be able to accomplish your goals. However, if you keep pondering what you can do and how to do it, those questions will eventually lead you to the answers you seek. It's fascinating to witness someone else's outstanding performance and think it's meant only for them, but if you invest in yourself and have faith in your abilities, you'll open doors and pave the way for countless achievements. Opportunities come our way, and it all depends on what we're willing to give.

Our lives hold different worth to others, and if you haven't yet cultivated self-love or don't believe you're capable of something great, it doesn't reflect your true potential. Your attitude affects everything you do, and a negative mindset can be draining. Honesty with yourself may reveal the pain of not getting the best out of life. Perhaps you're trying to be strong, and resilience can carry us far, but we can't be tough forever.

During your journey, you may find yourself weary from the hardships you face and yearning for happiness. It's important not to settle for less than what you deserve. If things aren't going well, there's no reason to continue down that path. The purpose of life is to seek joy and pleasure. You should realize this quickly before you lose motivation.

Although it's essential not to be swayed by every distraction along the way, there comes a point when you must leave the past behind and strive for success. That's why we are who we are; we prioritize prosperity and should pursue it relentlessly, even when faced with numerous distractions.

As you progress along your journey and grow each day, your success becomes crucial. Life can withhold essential elements of happiness if you're not on the right track. Once this pattern starts, it's challenging to change, and you may feel as if you're running out of time. Things can lose their meaning, and you might find yourself trapped in your own thoughts, struggling to regain control of your life.

Take pride in yourself, even if your unique perspective is hard for others to grasp. It's vital that it makes sense to you; the rest will follow. Lead others to understand your ideas, but don't break down before you reach the end of your journey. Ultimately, what you know and understand is your truth, the guiding principle that defines you.

We're all different, and we face significant challenges on our paths to understanding. Not everyone will relate to what you do, and that's okay. Each person has their beliefs and realities. What truly matters is your well-being, even if circumstances push you to your limits. In the end, you must choose yourself.

Beginnings have their origins somewhere, and you might have commenced your journey from a different point. Much of what initiates these beginnings are our intentions and desires. Perhaps you aspired to embody beauty and become a meaningful part of our world, which perpetually seeks individuals to fill the void that surrounds us.

Although we often lack comprehensive self-awareness and understanding of the universe, your journey could have taken various paths, and circumstances can have a significant influence on us, making it challenging to break free from their grasp. They seek devoted followers, those who immerse themselves in their pursuits. Occasionally, amidst the acknowledgment of external influences, it's crucial to initiate positive actions and witness their growth into life.

When you dedicate yourself to a particular cause, life springs forth from it, and our explorations of self never result in losses. If you commit to doing what is right, those intentions will guide your journey. For someone who dedicates their life to uncovering the truths of the universe, the world will eventually forget your initial lack of understanding and past mistakes.

The path ahead is unpredictable and fraught with potential missteps. Yet, there exists a threshold where you must begin expanding your comprehension of your surroundings to navigate accurately. At this juncture, you must choose to forge a meaningful existence, for there's a point of no return. Your decisions from there onwards hold the utmost significance.

Faith remains an elusive concept, impossible to measure definitively or quantify precisely. We are left at the end of the day with the need to cling to our identity. We find purpose in the belief that by pursuing virtuous goals with a benevolent heart, we can foster growth and create a meaningful life.

No matter how trapped we may sometimes feel, it's important to understand that you shouldn't be held accountable for things that don't truly represent your values. We all aspire to leave a lasting legacy, and it's crucial to recognize that our actions today will eventually catch up with us. You cannot simply live in any way that pleases you without consequences. Your present choices will undoubtedly impact the person you become in the future. Therefore, it's essential to strive for positive actions in the present, with the hope that, regardless of the weight of our past, we will reap the benefits in the future.

Living a life where you only expect to experience what you love about yourself is the path to success. Success is achieved when you invest your efforts in what truly matters to you. We invest in our future because, so far, we haven't achieved anything of which we can be proud. This realization stares back at us when we evaluate ourselves, often leaving us dissatisfied. We can only regret not taking more proactive steps to prevent these setbacks, regardless of our current circumstances. Investing in the present, even when we haven't done much good in the past, is the key to a brighter future.

So, how can we accelerate the process of creating a better life? Should we simply turn a blind eye to our shortcomings and focus solely on our strengths? Indeed, directing our attention towards our dreams becoming reality is vital for shaping our future selves. Approaching life in this way, where we feel deserving and successful, can cause the burdens of our past to fade away. As we embrace this new perspective, we witness the emergence of a fresh start and a brighter tomorrow.

Traveling the journey of life, you may have found yourself lost without realizing that there's justice for many aspects of our existence. Numerous circumstances may have burdened you more than you comprehend. These situations often cloud the connection between the present, the past, and the future. Sometimes, you might make choices based on your current circumstances without grasping how the present unfolded. Instead of gathering your thoughts and finding a way out of your predicament to ensure a better future, you may unknowingly persist in dragging yourself down.

The crux of the matter lies in our pursuit of a future we cherish, for life revolves around embracing what's to come. An essential realization involves acknowledging moments when we've been less than careful in our actions. The preceding events that led you to your current state are inconsequential compared to the potential for change. If your current situation doesn't suit you, you possess the power to transform it into something you adore about life.

It's gratifying to know that you've given your all to become the person you've aspired to be. Conversely, when you haven't consciously contributed positively to your life, you might find yourself in a cycle of negativity without understanding how you've perpetuated it. The positive resolution you seek may be intended for the future, but it requires proactive effort. Even if it demands your unwavering dedication, consider what you'd live your entire life for. Is it preferable to endure perpetual turmoil when, at some point, you could have altered your trajectory and harnessed your knowledge for good? Regardless of the perceived challenges or sacrifices, when achieving your desired outcome appears daunting, how will you respond? Are you hesitant to embrace change?

You may have heard that having faith can bring you the rewards you desire. Sometimes, it's not clear if you're fully aware of what you're doing, but doubts can still challenge your faith in yourself and the world. Despite your efforts to escape, things may not improve, and you might feel powerless. Instant solutions may be elusive.

However, remember that everything we experience is part of this life's test. Life won't test you beyond its own limits. So, keep faith, knowing you'll endure even during the most unexpected tough times. This strengthens your ability to defend yourself and is based on your righteous actions. You're not offering emptiness but understanding, which can bring positivity into your life.

You desire a great life and a brighter future, but current situations look bleak. No matter your efforts, they worsen, and you wonder if you've done something terribly wrong. However, we're rarely as guilty as we're made to believe. Sometimes, a small mistake lingers, and we're unsure how much good is needed for life to forgive our misunderstandings.

Choose to be a solution for your own progress. You've invested a lot in yourself, and your success is crucial. You possess creative knowledge, so work toward a solution. It may not change the present, but the future can be brighter, aligning with your well-being.

Chapter Three

Living under pressure

No matter which path you choose to follow in life, it's crucial to remain loyal to your journey. Your path may lead you to different places, but it's essential to understand where you are and what needs to be accomplished. Along the way, it's possible to lose touch with life and feel like you've failed or invested in something that won't set you free to become what you aspire to be. Sometimes, we lack the necessary motivation, which can significantly impact your progress.

While the world keeps moving forward on its own course, you are not lost. You may not always fit the mold of what everyone expects, but that's okay. Your goals are unique to your own path, and no one can prevent them from becoming a reality at some point in your life. Good things can happen, and that's what defines us as human beings—following our individual paths during different phases of life.

Having goals can sometimes make you feel like you're burdened by the human experience, as life's challenges may test your sense of normality. However, it's possible that everyone is seeking the same ultimate ingredient for happiness, which is being a human being in the present moment, alongside others. While your journey may have its challenges, it doesn't mean you're worthless;

you're still alive and evolving.

Many times, you may question whether you are right or wrong. In reality, you might not be mistaken; perhaps you simply haven't considered what you need to do. It's a good time to reflect on where you currently stand in your life's journey. Comparing your past, present, and future can provide valuable insights. By examining where you've come from and where you are now, you can gain a deeper understanding of yourself. If you're content with your current situation and your future aligns with your plans, you're on the right path. This is when you truly comprehend your purpose.

We often have clear visions of what we want to achieve, but these ideas come with the responsibility of success. You must work diligently to defend your beliefs and feel a sense of belonging to your ideals. Remember, failure doesn't necessarily mean you're completely wrong; it often results from succumbing to others' influences. View yourself as a unique individual responsible for your success in every aspect of life. Believe in your abilities and know that achieving your goals is possible without relying on others.

Sometimes, you may start from a disadvantaged position only to realize the importance of trusting your own judgment. Your life could have been significantly better if you had more faith in yourself. We tend to let our current circumstances cloud our judgment, but don't allow your situation to confuse you to the point of hopelessness. Be honest with your creative abilities and recognize that you are not left behind; you have the potential to change your life.

In life and love, there are moments when you might feel abandoned or under attack due to your thoughts. These situations can greatly impact your self-assurance as you navigate life based on your beliefs. Confidence plays a significant role in how you perceive your capabilities, potentially leading to self-doubt and feelings of unworthiness, especially when pursuing ambitious goals. This emotional turmoil can persist, causing you to contemplate giving up, which contradicts the spirit of innovation.

If your aspirations remain unattained, it's like losing a battle rather than emerging victorious. Your efforts should yield tangible results and positively affect your life. Your actions should not inadvertently harm your well-being or health due to a misguided belief in their rightness. Sometimes, we convince ourselves that a particular path is the only way to achieve our desired outcomes. Remember, true understanding is validated by fulfilling our commitments.

As you persist, others begin to recognize your purpose and its potential impact on their lives. Your determination becomes evident, and you make progress toward fulfilling your promises, both to yourself and fellow humans. We mustn't compromise the commitments we make, as failing to do so can alter the course of our lives in ways we never intended.

When you start something incorrectly, it can be challenging to make it right. Life often reflects how we approach it. Our errors and mistakes can disrupt the course of our lives. Sometimes, it's our own choices that hinder our progress, preventing us from leading fulfilling and happy lives.

To navigate the world, you must be mindful of potential challenges, weaknesses, and obstacles that might hinder your path. Situations can turn against you, especially if you lack experience. Your ability to thrive hinges on your depth of knowledge, and time plays a crucial role in testing the significance of your ideas.

People and their understanding of life are distinct entities. Time assesses the impact we have on others' lives and distinguishes those who leave a lasting mark. Carelessness can lead to underestimating project durations, jeopardizing our pursuit of perfection. As you work towards your goals, it's essential to consider time's substantial influence on your success, happiness, and love.

Time can pose a significant threat, forcing you to earn recognition for your skills. It can help you establish a robust reputation and cultivate enduring relationships with others who embrace your ideas, welcoming you into their hearts with love.

Think about how important time can be in shaping your life. Your thoughts and ideas can gain recognition and value. If you view every opportunity as a chance to learn more about life, it won't be a weakness. It becomes something significant and meaningful to live for, as talents often find a place in people's hearts, becoming timeless gifts.

Your life's quality hinges on your love for it, your passion for creation, and your dedication to your talents. Do you care about the world and the special things that make us who we are? Regardless of the time and effort it takes, even if achieving your goals is challenging, pushing through and showing everyone your progress can lead to a fulfilling life and deep understanding.

The truth is, it might take a bit longer. We face daily challenges, but with persistence, dreams can become reality. It may seem unbelievable, but if you continue to explore your creativity and strive to be the best, you'll realize that faith is the key to unlocking your innermost desires. We are valuable, and life is not meant to be filled with endless suffering. Something is meant to discover us, and our unique perspective on the universe.

Somehow, there's something that will satisfy the eagerness deep within you. It will help you understand various aspects of life. Sometimes, life might seem really tough, and you might feel like celebrating the life you have isn't important. But remember, it will matter when the time comes.

This unexpected moment could arrive when you least anticipate it. Often, things seem unclear when you're just starting your journey. Even if you look ahead and feel like giving up because you can't see how it's all possible, imagine if this was your only path. What would you do in such a situation? You might question your ability to reach your destination because, so far, it seems unreachable.

However, consider this: You might be testing the waters, but when you truly desire something, mere testing isn't enough to survive. That's because many things can disrupt our lives and steal away the comfort we're used to. The years we're supposed to spend without worries turn into hard work. Even if you worry, who can make those worries disappear? This is the reality we must embrace.

We're human because we have desires to fulfill. Only then can we find contentment in ourselves. Our goals become the primary purpose of our lives, the main obstacle between us and success. Don't be ashamed of the journey you've undertaken and the challenges you've faced. Instead, be glad that you've grown and matured through it all.

When you embrace the path of self-discovery and seek to distinguish yourself, many revelations will unfold before you. Allowing yourself the necessary time for personal growth will transform even the most daunting challenges into manageable endeavors. Furthermore, existing threats will gradually fade, ushering in a fresh chapter in your life. These are the opportunities that should always be eagerly anticipated; do not let them slip through your grasp. Stay vigilant and maintain focus on the unique opportunities designed to lead you to success.

The key distinction lies within yourself, perhaps in the way you perceive and operate within the world. While you aspire to achieve your life's desires, various obstacles may slow your progress, making you hesitant and apprehensive. Your greatest strength can sometimes transform into your Achilles' heel in the vast landscape of life, leaving you feeling unprepared for the challenges reality presents. Nevertheless, each day, you grow stronger, and the monumental barriers before you and your destiny can be scaled with the unwavering dedication of your heart, mind, and soul.

Life sometimes offers shortcuts that may seem tempting, but they aren't always the best choice, especially if you want to be responsible. It's important to consider how you achieve success because it can profoundly affect your journey. You can't just take advantage of every opportunity; instead, you should stay focused on your ultimate goal. This focused approach can have a positive impact on who you are as a person.

While there are many external influences, you've also nurtured your inner self, and not everything in the world is meant for you to use. It might not align with who you truly are. To navigate life successfully, you must develop your understanding and perspective on various aspects of life and love. This is something everyone worries about because, regardless of your background, there's something you still seek.

Life can throw formidable challenges at us, making it difficult to find peace with our circumstances. The path you've chosen might not always lead you to where you want to be. Therefore, it's crucial to become the person who can truly shape your desired outcomes.

There are times when setbacks can make you contemplate giving up on your dreams, your unique ideas, and your way out of challenges. We often hesitate to expand our horizons due to fear. Your current circumstances may confine you, but your mind has the potential to transcend those limitations and guide you toward the right path. Something within you can ignite and drive your progress. So, when considering your own creations, don't worry too much about when they will achieve success. Focus on the journey and your personal growth instead.

You need life to come alive, and witness its emergence because, in the face of daily challenges, our minds are like personal investments. They should take center stage in our lives. If you believe in achieving the ultimate reward, have faith in your ability to do so. The passage of time shouldn't concern you, even if you've devoted your life to a particular idea for success.

How do you react to adversity along your journey? Does it have a strong grip on you, potentially weighing you down to your lowest point? There are stages you must traverse to become the person you aspire to be. You must dedicate yourself fully and witness a lifetime crafted from your own comprehension—a level of self-contentment.

Live life as you've envisioned it, with your most significant decisions blossoming into creative ventures that shape your daily existence. You're determined to grasp the essence of your actions. Intentions are always present, and you may be right or wrong, but this is an idea you're committed to getting right, whether it's for personal gain or out of sheer passion. Now, it has become your entire existence—an idea poised to draw everything you need from this world, ultimately crafting your happiness.

If you lack the courage to continue shaping your life along the path you've chosen, it's a sign that you lack the motivation to achieve your desired objectives. Your goal lies deep within you, akin to that last shred of self-assurance residing within. If you genuinely aspire to construct a solid foundation with a sterling reputation, you mustn't shy away from making sacrifices, shedding your old self, and embracing the emergence of something new. Tap into the depths of your soul, unveil the person residing within, and muster unwavering determination from within yourself. You must embark on the journey to sustain your livelihood, working diligently until all threats to your progress dissipate.

Throughout your life, you've been on a quest to discover your true self, even in the most dire circumstances. Now, you have a splendid opportunity to unearth your authentic identity and embark on a clear path towards fulfilling your long-held dreams and lifelong objectives. This is a period where you can harness both financial and physical gains from your endeavors; you've given yourself ample time to witness your efforts materialize.

While much in life can be rationalized, you can no longer make peace with waiting for something that remains unreal. You yearn to witness everything spring to life. The worthiness of one's idea is defined by the objectives one holds dear and the outcomes anticipated with utmost passion.

What is it that you aim to achieve, and where must you arrive? The world serves as a platform for genuine love, and only what you ardently desire will come to fruition. You possess the capacity to become absolutely anything you need to be, but you must do your part and allow it to govern the core of your inner self. Your past may attempt to ensnare you in its depths, but you must introspect and ask yourself whether you'll allow it to rule or forever mar your life.

How can you overcome challenging situations and difficulties that you face? If you can't turn these challenges into goals and dreams, your life might not turn out as you wish. You must set yourself free and make your life become a reality. Even when you experience delays, remember that they won't last forever. In the end, you'll be able to say that you've learned how to achieve success, and this will bring you the satisfaction you desire.

When you feel pressure pushing you to realize that you haven't reached your goals yet, and you're stuck where you are, don't let it permanently bring you down. Instead, find the determination to lead you forward. Let determination guide you through all obstacles, and you'll see your life take shape. If you've identified your goal as the most important thing in your life, then work towards it. Don't let questions like "how," "what," and "why" trap you in a world of doubt. You can either waste your life by being different from who you want to be or let yourself be saved by true dedication.

Remember, the entire human race is counting on you, and it's clear that you can't be anything else. Don't allow negativity to persuade you otherwise; it shouldn't come and undermine the solid foundation you've built. Strengthen your resolve with deep commitment, as this is what distinguishes people and allows you to grow beyond your limits.

If necessary, make a positive impact on others' lives. Helping someone or healing an individual can lead to lasting relationships and a sense of worthiness. Many will hold you in high regard, and you'll grow together, never facing difficulties or seemingly impossible tasks alone.

Throughout our lives, our intentions and the quality of our work speak volumes about who we are and what we represent. In the end, people will appreciate you for the person you've become. Even during moments of self-doubt, your unique qualities will shine through. You'll hold a special place in people's hearts, and although they might find it challenging to fully understand you, there's something about your essence that lingers in their souls like a work of art.

In this world, there must be something we find joy in. From what we know, the universe has the power to set us free. You cannot be excluded from being normal; it's who you are and the path you've chosen. Although obstacles may attempt to hold you back, the world is not against you.

Even in moments of uncertainty, knowledge will often come to your aid, propelling you forward in life. It's important to remember that people are at the heart of everything we do. Our connection with others goes beyond our personal preferences; it's a universal truth that everyone eventually comprehends and finds their place within.

People always play a significant role in our endeavors. Never underestimate the importance of individuals in your journey. Keep them as your primary focus, allowing them to discover their true selves and relate to their unique circumstances.

Never forget that people are the core of our pursuits. With this understanding as your guiding principle, you can venture as far as the universe permits. Embrace this perspective, and you'll never feel lost. If challenges arise, do it for the people, work to gain their acceptance. Mastering your understanding requires accepting people as they are, supporting them, and providing a space for their growth within your creations.

Life can sometimes bring sadness due to the path you've chosen. It may seem as if your initial life had all the answers, while the current one lacks an understanding of how to coexist with others. Perhaps you feel you've deviated from your intended path. However, competition will always be present. To be truly loved and appreciated by others, you must stand out and be unique in some way.

Recognize the significance of working for and being understood by people. They want to feel included in everything you do, even when it's not solely about you. Avoid building your ideas solely on fantasy; reality is what we all need at various points in life. Understand that we all have the potential to excel, but it won't happen by chance; it will be the result of your intentions. Your eagerness to achieve will be evident to all, as everything you do is directed toward their understanding.

Overcoming ignorance is one of the most challenging tasks you can undertake. It's crucial not to turn a blind eye to anything. The things you choose to ignore today can eventually return to haunt you and cause harm. Regardless of your chosen path, whether it's in the realm of creation or contributing to the world's development, embracing creativity and a life that resonates with others is vital. While many distractions in the world aim to limit our true potential, they can also weaken us over time.

To truly understand what you need to become, wholehearted dedication to greatness is essential. If you aspire to be the best at what you do, you must give your all, leaving nothing outside that path. Our ideas reflect our identity and values, especially our authentic ones. You may strive to stand out and be extraordinary, but your work will ultimately stand as a living testament to your life's purpose.

Perhaps you lack the knowledge required, but with love and a commitment to excellence, your inner strength will shine through. It's our passion for everything we embody that weaves the fabric of our hearts, shielding us from the bitterness that can tear our souls apart. If you're unsure of your direction, you may miss out on the opportunity to extend a healing hand to others in their times of need.

Instill a culture of values that celebrate being exceptional and remarkable. How can you lead a life entirely rooted in these values if you don't fully grasp their significance? Even when the world exerts pressure on you, strive for equilibrium and resist complete surrender.

Many individuals with brilliant ideas fail to bring their visions to life because they neglect the crucial aspect of interacting with fellow humans and making them connect with their concepts. They rush and don't allow themselves sufficient time to be understood by others, succumbing to external influences that steer them away from their chosen path.

If you had allowed more love into your interactions with people, you might have secured a lasting place in their lives. Your passion for your work could have enabled you to thrive, but challenging circumstances caused some to give up. They struggled to find the affection needed to carve out a special spot in the hearts of those who relied on their assistance to achieve their dreams. Don't deny yourself and your ideas; don't doubt whether you still possess the excitement required for life.

To enable creativity to flow through you, genuine love sustains our ideas eternally. Whatever hardships you face should be a reflection of the person you must be when dealing with people. This should remain your core focus on your journey, prioritizing it above all else, especially when the opportunity arises.

You may have experienced numerous trials, but don't let pressure stifle your capacity to love. Keep your central focus intact so you can realize the future of your creation. Since our intentions define our best selves, there's no reason to move forward if you've abandoned caring. Remember the purpose behind your creation; moving forward, you can express your thoughts, but to triumph over all obstacles, preserve the very reason you pursued your objective.

When you ultimately succeed, let it be with a deep devotion to humanity at the core of all your endeavors, and nothing will diminish that. In the end, it will speak volumes about your character. What attempts to deter you on your journey is the essence of who you are before reaching your destination, and it can accompany you for a considerable time.

It's not like you have many opportunities to change things, you only get one chance to be the best and do what's right, no matter what challenges you face. Stick to who you are or what you know, and your intentions won't be permanently damaged. Avoid tarnishing your values, because anyone can shape themselves through your influence if you empower them.

Always remember the people you're dedicated to serving throughout your life. If you show them love, they'll surprise you because they care deeply about you too. We all face struggles in our lives, and many care about you just as much as you hold them close to your heart. They'll guide you through tough times and help your empire succeed. Don't let them down; they'll never disappoint you. They'll offer you endless opportunities and bring happiness into your life.

Keep them in your heart, and let love be the driving force in everything you do. As challenging as it can be to shine brightly in a world that often forgets the importance of serving human needs, you embody true love. You won't go unnoticed if you prioritize people in your heart; they'll show you how much they love you in return. Let them matter and influence your decisions; you don't want to lose your connection with them. Even though we may live in different worlds, there's something common among us, and that's what truly matters in our lives.

Chapter Four

Win it the other way around

You might believe that taking the easiest path is the best way, but sometimes, life demands more from us, and we can't possibly know everything. Experience is crucial, and we must dabble in various aspects of our lives. It's rare to get everything right on the first try, and most people can attest to this truth. Comfort isn't always achievable right away.

You can grapple with challenges for a while or continue searching in circles, trying to find your way, but the journey isn't always smooth. When you venture into the world, be prepared. Remember, you have a unique aspiration in life, and it's not that you lack talent; your life just hasn't aligned with your goals yet. You're in a transitional phase, practicing how to seize every opportunity effectively.

As you strive to shine, don't just prepare for fleeting chances. Learn to sustain yourself during periods when you won't see immediate results. The concept of "struggle" or "hustle" can be ambiguous, signifying the relentless pursuit of your goals, even when you're uncertain about the way forward. However, ensure your efforts align with your values and don't compromise your integrity.

Despite your diligent preparation, success may remain elusive, leading you to question what separates you from the millions who thrive daily. You might experience moments of envy because your life is evolving, but something must be sufficient for you to progress.

Aside from love, life can pose numerous challenges that may seem insurmountable, and the path to clarity isn't always clear. Answers may reside within us, yet translating them into action proves daunting. You might feel hindered by a desire for leisure.

Do we need to consider changing our perspective and start thinking of our career as something we are willing to do whatever it takes to succeed in? Because treating it like a mere hobby won't lead us anywhere. Perhaps this shift in mindset could prove more effective, granting us the determination to overcome the challenges that have held sway over our lives for so long. If this mindset shift still doesn't yield the desired results, it may be time to reevaluate everything, as it no longer serves any purpose.

Consider this: the life you believe to be the ideal one might not necessarily materialize, and you may find yourself waiting for it to become meaningful, only to realize it never does. Clinging to a future that may never come to pass becomes increasingly difficult, even if it has become your sole aspiration.

So, why turn away from it? Is it not akin to undergoing a process like male circumcision, where you endure pain initially but then invest the necessary time in healing? Eventually, you emerge liberated, and that's all it takes to attain the best that life has to offer. Perhaps it demands a temporary sacrifice—forgetting about many things and dedicating yourself wholeheartedly to the task, rather than clinging to outdated notions and concepts that no longer define who we are. Push forward with unwavering determination if this has indeed become the life you yearn for.

Must your focus be exclusively fixed on a single ambition when you can accumulate a wealth of knowledge that contributes to your overarching goal? Some of us rely heavily on various facets of life, and if you discover an optimal path forward, why not embrace it wholeheartedly if it yields the desired results?

Occasionally, all it takes is becoming a part of a supportive community. Once you've uncovered a breakthrough, transitioning to something else becomes more manageable. You may not have anticipated the challenges you'd face, only to find yourself grappling with something that never grants you true freedom. So, if you get it right the first time, consider yourself fortunate for dedicating your life to something worthy of your efforts.

We all make mistakes in life, but it's essential to make decisions and avoid things that aren't worth our attention. If you're not benefiting, and there's nothing holding you back but yourself, then it's time to act for your own sake. Even though the past may tug at you, dwelling on it doesn't make us stronger; instead, it weakens us. Our character is shaped by honesty and staying true to our aspirations, often requiring loyalty as we move forward.

While you might deceive the world, it's much harder to deceive yourself. True devotion is the only fair way forward. So, cease treating yourself as unworthy. Take just a minute of your life to look far ahead and genuinely commit to it; don't pretend to look there. This is the time when you must keep moving.

Splitting your attention isn't the solution; you must acknowledge that without prioritization, you'll remain stagnant. Remember, you're not holding anyone back, even when others use dishonest tactics to advance. Your commitment to fairness is your strength. Recognize the value of your life as a precious gift, and through focused efforts towards greater achievements, you will reach beautiful destinations. There are moments when you must rely solely on your own determination and love for everything you are. In those moments, you can chart your own course and achieve the seemingly impossible, despite others' doubts.

The constant drive to do what's right might make you question whom you serve with these principles. But these values protect you and your interests. If you ever wonder why you must continue doing good, it could be because you're serving the honesty within you. When the path isn't straightforward, and you're tempted to take shortcuts, the inner conflict you experience becomes a test of your faith.

It's ironic how you once felt compelled to do right all the time, and now you're facing the initial challenges of what you once hoped to achieve. Who are you trying to convince with the life you lead? It's no longer about impressing others but living the life you envisioned. Your purpose is to journey down the unique path that you can no longer substitute for anything else.

Truthfulness is a unique and fascinating journey to embark upon, wherein your current self differs from the person you'll discover along the way. Numerous surprises await, each presenting a life-altering question, forcing you to distinguish between these realms of existence. As you hang in the balance, contemplating the never-ending adventure, consider whether you can resist any obstacle.

Embrace that narrow gateway that many overlook. As you become candid with yourself, assess your determination and commitment towards your aspirations, understanding their significance and discarding frivolities. Take a courageous stride towards your desired future. If wholehearted success is your aim, temporarily shelve present pleasures that might obstruct your path. Traverse the unwavering route of determination until prosperity molds your endeavors. Wholehearted dedication entails minimal risk but promises a sturdy foundation for the future.

In a world filled with deceit, prioritize honesty amidst the chaos, working diligently to establish a virtuous path forward. Generosity should replace mere taking; giving holds an intrinsic richness. By opening your heart, you reveal your deepest desires, allowing others to fulfill them.

Picture your most profound needs met, and contemplate what you desire above all else, the yearning you are eager to satisfy, transcending all else within you. This is how we achieve fulfillment in every aspect of our lives. It underscores the importance of honesty with ourselves, reminding us not to pursue goals that lack intrinsic value. Authenticity prevents self-deception and, through the practice of life's virtues, offers a meaningful return that aligns with your deepest desires.

Therefore, let your pursuit of your goals rank high among your life's ambitions.

There's a great deal to be gained from giving with love, and you can indeed build your path to success around this principle. Instead of taking from others and assuming they won't understand your actions, consider giving wholeheartedly. By doing so, you'll witness the road ahead clear itself just as it should. Refraining from giving is considered a wrongdoing and a burden. Staying in one spot while the rest of the world moves forward reveals your true desires for life. Therefore, learn to give generously, even when you're in dire straits. Don't withhold your contributions, as this is how you find your place in the universe.

Giving abundantly is a means of personal growth; it reflects who you are. This practice can be applied to any endeavor or passion. Embrace the act of giving in love, life, work, and all facets of existence. Your desires will manifest as you give freely, allowing you to progress more effectively than if you only focus on taking. Don't resent it when there comes a time when you need to pour yourself out; instead, embrace it. Keep giving, even when circumstances are challenging or life is tough to handle.

When you give generously, unnecessary obstacles will move out of your path, and the world will welcome you with open arms. As you decrease your self-importance, the divine increases in your life. No matter how talented you may be, you still require the blessings and support of others to advance in certain stages of life. Don't hold back your potential; cultivate what you have within you. Don't hesitate to offer your gifts, as this is how you propel your creativity forward. Whether you possess extraordinary talent or only sheer determination, you'll never know unless you're given an opportunity, and that chance could come from someone unexpected.

You should think about your point of view, which is what sets you apart from others. Do you see the world differently from others, or do you focus on your interests, or what everyone else sees? This can help you better understand yourself, what influences your perspective, is it love or hate? This can guide you to reconnect with yourself, to clearly grasp what makes everything possible, what turns dreams into reality.

We all have goals that make us unique, but what if your desires don't align with how things should be? You may have relied too much on other people to help you achieve your goals, and they aren't always available. When they don't meet your expectations, you can feel lost because the path is uncertain.

Things might take a negative turn, and you might face setbacks, not just for a day but for a long time, and you need that goal to materialize. It could be the only thing standing between you and the life you want. We can become consumed by these dreams and lose touch with ourselves, which can be destructive if we're not careful. We yearn for more in our lives, not because we're failing entirely, but because we're still struggling to understand the path ahead.

You may have thought things would go as planned, but then you realize your hopes didn't materialize as expected, and you need to adapt to new, challenging circumstances. If you've been aiming for success and part of that journey is uncomfortable, what would you do? Such challenges can arise unexpectedly, requiring you to do things that aren't easy to get where you want to be. How would you adjust to that? Sometimes, it's the sacrifices we make that pave the way to achieving our hopes and dreams as they should be.

Sometimes, you may encounter challenges on your journey, and it might seem like your efforts aren't leading you to your destination. However, there's always another route to explore. It's clear that you can lose your way and forget what you've learned, making it hard to grasp things through that particular path. Nevertheless, humans are never completely clueless. What does it say about you if you never discover something within yourself that's more valuable than your current state? We often lose our present selves because a greater world beckons.

What often propels individuals to fame isn't solely their academic knowledge but rather their ability to uncover hidden potential and bring it to light. There's usually a catalyst that drives you to realize your full potential when other avenues have failed. You must have faith in yourself and acknowledge that you are not a failure.

We've all followed a certain path, striving for success, and when it doesn't pan out as expected, we embrace a new cause, which often becomes the key to success. Over time, as you mature and gain experience, you learn from your mistakes and avoid repeating them. The truth is, you can never have a precise roadmap to achieve your life's desires.

There's always a gap between what we desire and how to attain it. When the "how" becomes perplexing, you must contemplate what you truly need and how to attain it. Finding the connection between these two concepts will pave the way to your ultimate goal, ideally at an early stage in your life's journey.

You might feel excited about what you aspire to become or what it reflects about your character. However, as time pushes you to your limits, you may find yourself pondering the consequences of unmet needs. It can lead to a sense of desperation, a feeling of being irrevocably lost. We often yearn for so much, yet achieving our desires doesn't always happen when we expect it to. This can lead to a profound dissatisfaction with our lives. It's true that we bear responsibility for our failures and successes, but when you reach a point where you're unsure about your next move, you might yearn for external support focused on our well-being and progress, which unfortunately seems absent.

If you've never experienced the disappointment of being denied something you deeply cherish, you may think it's unrelated. However, it's interconnected. Before embarking on a journey, we rarely know for certain that we'll be on our own. You may wish for a place where you can entrust all your desires, but such a place may not exist in the life we lead today. Things are no longer as they once were, and the feeling of isolation can be overpowering. If the concept of placing your trust in an external entity doesn't align with your lifestyle, you might feel excluded.

If you persist in maintaining this mindset, you risk losing more than you gain, as you allow something to control your life from the start. By adopting a proactive stance and relying on your own capabilities, you can transform into a shining star, pursuing your goals without relying on miracles or external forces. We compete based on what we know and our own abilities.

Have you ever thought about the path you're traveling on and where it might lead you? Is it taking you to the same place you had hoped for, or do you find yourself a bit lost along the way? Sometimes, when we can't have what we want, it can feel like our world has crumbled from deep within, and we can clearly see how it has disrupted our life. It's like we're haunted by our desire to achieve more, but at the end of the day, we feel stuck because it hasn't taken us anywhere significant.

It might have all started as a childhood dream, and you became so determined to reach those goals that you're still holding onto them, even if they're not bringing you any real benefits. You keep pursuing something without knowing what you'll gain from it, but it's evident that it's not helping you now, and it remains unfulfilled deep within your heart. You once aspired to become something, but for a long time, it's just been holding your life in one place. Now, it's time to make a decision about which part of your life you should let go of and focus on one goal that truly matters to you. You can dedicate yourself wholeheartedly to something, whether it's ordinary or extraordinary, as long as it's meaningful to you.

This is the moment in your life when you need to turn away from things that no longer serve you and have faith in something that brings you pride. Uncertainty about what to do can lead to mistakes, so sometimes, you have to make sacrifices to give life meaning. You might find yourself in challenging situations, where some things happen by chance, while others require your determination to make them happen. It's all about applying your knowledge and skills in practical ways to achieve your dreams.

You're not stuck on everything. From all that you've come to understand, you can push yourself forward in the direction of your creativity. Even though you can't see where it will lead to success from where you stand, you must have faith in yourself if it means a lot to you.

Consider this: whether you stay in one place, you'll never find true happiness until you have your own place, and you're unsure about how that will happen. The future won't harm you; it will bring change. You're only confined by the present moment, and the length of time it takes to act on your dreams doesn't matter. What truly counts is that you waited for your deepest desires and finally pursued them.

You can set high goals in life, or life can aim back at you, causing you to lose sight of who you are until you begin to dislike yourself. When you fail to fulfill your life's needs, you might start believing that something is fundamentally wrong with you because there's no one to provide the love you seek.

Ask yourself: "How can I become what I need?" Make changes in your life when you strive for a better direction. When you've been trying hard, you can't predict where one opportunity might lead. Understand what you're truly working for and how to achieve it with precision. Even if it takes a while, once you get it right, you'll experience freedom as it opens numerous doors. These are rare skills to possess, but once you have them, you become a valuable asset. Maybe your initial efforts didn't go well, but this kind of understanding will guide you to a beautiful destination. Nurture it to grow.

As we journey through life, we often experience losses and change who we are. It doesn't have to be this way, but sometimes we endure it. There's a part of ourselves we might try to escape, our old self, because we keep losing the familiar, and it can feel like our aspirations betray us. However, when we reflect on our journey, we begin to grasp why we embarked on it. We find purpose in striving for our desired self, contrasting it with who we didn't want to become. Even the challenges of sharing our ideas with the world can't deter us from our chosen path. We carry a sense of pride within us, and despite the difficulties, we remain certain that our life is on the right track, resisting the urge to change it.

Have you ever looked outside and felt envious? You might wonder why your current self hasn't taken you as far as you'd like and has caused setbacks in important areas. You attempt to make improvements, but the timing isn't right, and you know you deserve better. Deep down, you've gained insight that tells you that you're not where you should be. You question if your love for this world might be holding you back, restricting your potential.

Do you truly understand how to strike a balance in life so that you don't feel overwhelmed by every challenge that comes your way? Sometimes, certain situations require your comprehension to make sense, while other times, we find ourselves grappling with the pursuit of perfection. Perhaps, initially, we are challenged by our life goals, which often align with our aspirations but may not unfold as expected.

You can sense when you're engaged in a fierce internal struggle. The unpredictability of the difficulties that life presents can catch you off guard, leaving you with unfulfilled expectations. We tend to assume that reaching our desired destinations should happen quickly, but it's essential to acknowledge that life and love may knock us down repeatedly, making it tempting to compensate with alternative pursuits. However, this substitute may not genuinely represent love or a better life. Perhaps we stumble in executing our plans, not because we lack the capacity to know everything at once but because there is a vast amount of knowledge to acquire.

When you fully commit yourself to your objectives, you can pursue your passions without restraint. We often lose sight of our true selves along the journey to achieving lofty goals, rendering many things meaningless. This can lead to self-discontent, and coming to terms with these aspects of yourself can be challenging. Hoping for something different while accepting an undesirable reality can be a burdensome endeavor.

We don't simply engage in actions with the hope that they won't materialize into reality. Instead, we exert every conceivable effort within our grasp, dedicating our entire being to the cause, even when we find ourselves with nothing left to give. We might ponder the extensive cost of making our aspirations a tangible existence, pondering what we must sacrifice to breathe life into our own ideas. Do we merely pour our entire essence into it, hoping for a favorable outcome even if it ultimately fails? It's not just or equitable to create a space for disappointment in our lives. Subjecting oneself to such a circumstance is profoundly disheartening, and our aspirations shouldn't lead us down this path.

Is it disheartening when you commit your unwavering devotion to realizing a vision, or is the real shortcoming a lack of the inner courage needed to fulfill your purpose? Becoming accustomed to disappointment should not be your norm, as it will erode your sense of pride in extracting quality from life. You may attempt to reconcile with this reality, but you'll find it insurmountable. You can pray for a fresh start, but it may remain elusive, and this is where we risk losing ourselves—starting a journey but never reaching the destination. Only then does the magnitude of lost opportunities become painfully evident.

The crux of the matter lies in the possibility that one particular endeavor may have fallen short in the past, but there exists another avenue where you can achieve similar outcomes. What sets you apart is your discerning choice amidst myriad possibilities. There may have been a time when the most vital aspect of your life eluded you. However, even through that phase, you can attain the financial abundance you seek and everything that success promises to deliver. You can find the love you yearn for, in the manner you desire to be cherished, and all will be well. This treasure, once internalized, cannot be wrested from you. You have harbored this dream within you, and you rightfully deserve every offering that life extends to you, all without anyone ever fathoming the incredible journey that made it all possible.

Sometimes, what really counts is the end result rather than the way we got there. The journey might not have been all sunshine and roses; it could have been something you didn't particularly enjoy or wish to go through. But, it turned out to be essential in reaching your desired goals. You didn't foresee that it would also bring some hardships into your life, but now it's become the key to everything you've ever wanted. Sometimes, it doesn't matter how challenging the path seemed – in the end, you achieved your goals.

So, why spend your whole life regretting how it all unfolded? You reaped what you sowed, and more blessings came your way as a result. You've become someone special to yourself, and despite the obstacles that tried to derail your journey, you don't have to stay down forever. You altered the course of things and made something new happen.

In the past, you might not have been thrilled with where life was taking you, but the time has come for you to become someone you truly admire – someone you never knew you had the potential to be. Even though the journey might have been challenging and left you feeling lost at times, it would have been even sadder if you had pursued something only to realize at the end that it wasn't what you wanted. However, this journey became the life you needed, and you didn't return empty-handed; you came back with a trove of achievements. You've now embraced the truth that you wouldn't be content without realizing at least some of these dreams that have shaped your identity.

We can only offer so much of ourselves, and we must understand the significance of committing to our goals. The strength and energy we invest in achieving our desired objectives can sometimes leave us with nothing else to live for. It becomes the sole focus of our lives, and despite the potential setbacks,

50

you overcame them through sheer determination. That's the kind of resilience we reserve for the things we truly love, and it might leave us with little left to give to anything else. Once you decide to wholeheartedly pursue something, it can transform your life. You may face numerous challenges along the way, but you'll no longer belong to the place you left behind; a part of you must embrace leaving everything behind for good.

Chapter Five

What would you do?

The world has undergone significant modernization, bidding farewell to the old ways and embracing a new realm along with its influences. The transformation of our surroundings prompts us to reflect on the changes and our continued pursuit of our passions. However, many challenges still loom on the path to our deepest desires.

For those striving to ascend to the heights of success, they often ponder what it takes to gain acceptance from humanity. They grapple with questions about whether they measure up to society's expectations or if obstacles in their journey are tests of their dedication. Sometimes, it feels like hard work alone is insufficient, and opportunities slip through our grasp.

Once one has determined their ultimate aspiration, the burning passion within drives them relentlessly. They are willing to do whatever it takes to attain their goal. But what forces could stand in the way of realizing these dreams? What might impose limitations on their path to success?

It's challenging to fully commit to something that doesn't align with your inner vision. True contentment in success lies in being happy with who you are. This forms the foundation upon which we build our self-worth, allowing us to discover meaning in life and love, irrespective of the duration of our endeavors. Time can overshadow our essence, and without genuine value, we risk falling short of our aspirations. This loss feels akin to life being stolen from us, even though we possessed it all along. A solid foundation, however, stands as a steadfast source of happiness, motivating us to persevere even in the face of adversity.

However, if you consistently follow these principles, you will never find yourself lost, not even once. This journey may span an extended duration, but rest assured, you will attain mastery as intended, even during the challenging periods when it feels like you're struggling. As you work diligently toward becoming precisely what you desire, without a shred of doubt, remember that life won't pause to accommodate you if you haven't grasped your purpose. The key to unlocking opportunities lies in unwavering determination, granting you the freedom to pursue your passions in life. As you embark on this path and conquer the fears that may linger due to a lack of knowledge, you'll soon discover that much is at stake.

Foster trust in your judgment and have faith in your understanding of life, for this belief is your sole source of attaining what you require in life. Our needs are founded on the knowledge we possess, determining how far we can advance toward our goals and how we are perceived within the wider world. Remember, we all have choices, and you have consciously chosen the path you walk, defining the extent of your capacity to pursue your passions. This choice brings you a sense of tranquility as you witness the world's daily creation.

Irrespective of whether your experiences surpass or fall short of expectations, remember that quality emerges from patience. Believe unwaveringly in the life you have envisioned, and when you eventually arrive at your desired destination, recognize that it didn't occur by chance; it was the result of your resolute determination. You will arrive with a profound understanding and unwavering willpower.

By embracing these virtues, you'll come to realize that there's no need to mistreat yourself. When opportunities come your way, it's often because you actively sought them, and regardless of how others judge our choices, you inherently recognize your competence in your endeavors. You don't always require validation; your work can speak for itself. If you're honest with yourself, you'll never find yourself lost in any situation; instead, it becomes a canvas for your creativity to shine.

We are the architects of our ideas, and you must sow the seeds of knowledge that will yield eternal fruit. This is where you will reap the rewards throughout your life. To achieve your ambitions, you must face the world with a profound understanding. Amidst the struggles and pains, you'll eventually arrive at the point where knowledge liberates you. There may be moments when you feel that nothing can carry you beyond that threshold, as the world can ensnare you with its myriad distractions.

Many times, life might not offer immediate pleasures, especially when you're diligently working towards future goals where happiness will hold great significance. No one should suffer for their desires, as it's you who aspires to gain from your efforts. You may find yourself frustrated that others don't grasp your vision, goals, or ultimate objectives, yearning for the support you believe you deserve.

But consider, how can others provide the support you need when they don't fully comprehend your life's direction? Everyone possesses their unique perspective, and when it comes to visions, we often see different things, leading to diverse interpretations. It's clear why your journey depends on your efforts and your ability to prepare yourself for this journey of creativity, knowledge, and life.

Sometimes, you find yourself in a situation that you must tackle independently. You need to ponder and strategize to discover a simpler way to achieve your desires, no matter how seemingly impossible they appear. Consider this: If you truly desire something and there are no other options, what actions would you take? Recognize that much of your success depends on your understanding and the time you invest. Time becomes your greatest sacrifice, but it's essential to attain the quality required for your aspirations.

It's disheartening when you've pursued a lifelong passion longer than anything else, and you need to embody unwavering faith, the ultimate key to unlocking your full potential as a human being. It's this unwavering commitment in our pursuits that can guide us even through life's darkest moments. If you believe in your genius and intellect, no one can sway your conviction. Your task is to prove to yourself that you possess all the qualities necessary.

While it might not be a common goal among many, it's crucial for others to grasp and appreciate your values. People need to understand what you represent in life. Though we often cling to our past selves, there are moments that mirror our deep love for the world, encouraging us to let go of the past and embark on a fresh beginning.

Every person shares a common quality, even though we all have different goals in life. However, we can share a similar determination to achieve what we need. We often lack insight into what others know about life, as our understanding is shaped by their thoughts. It can be surprising to discover their perspectives, motivating us to improve our own thinking. It's essential to use your time wisely when contemplating your desires, as this will help you make the most of your knowledge. Regardless of your starting point in life, proper mental preparation leads to understanding your path.

You won't always feel completely stuck; sometimes, it's essential to allow life to flow and not be too stubborn. Prioritize what's necessary and create space for it. A breakthrough has a way of emerging from challenging situations. However, there are times when life's common struggles can hold it back for an extended period. Staying focused may require allowing things to unfold naturally, accepting them as they are meant to be. While some things may demand your effort to be part of your life, it's also essential to learn when to adapt.

You shouldn't permanently damage your heart. There are things that are not currently a part of your life, but you require them, such as love. Real love demands patience, even though we often find it hard to wait for things to align perfectly because we desire them immediately. The time you spend with someone cannot be shortened beyond the present, and our physical desires are evident. Occasionally, you require someone to be ordinary and to care about other things. This reveals the deep-seated need for compassion within us.

When something presents a significant challenge, requiring all your efforts and creativity, you may strive to find a path forward, yet not achieve success. In such cases, it may not be the right fit for you, and persisting may not be in your best interest. If something aligns with your lifelong purpose, you may encounter struggles on your journey to perfection, while being deeply considered. Life grants us the will to pursue our passions, and the remainder involves pushing ourselves to excel and outshine others.

This will serves as your initial step along a particular path that many might shy away from due to its perceived difficulty. By honing your skills and avoiding subpar performance, you can sidestep potential humiliation since people are quick to judge. Ultimately, your image stands on the line, awaiting judgment from others. If your abilities are lacking, you may squander your time when honesty with oneself could have led to thriving and achieving one's full potential.

While each of us has a unique place where we belong, the diverse ways we engage with the world contribute to its extraordinary nature. If we comprehended everything about life, the world would lose its charm and cease to be an enchanting place to reside. We coexist, each with distinct talents, to shape reality as it was meant to be. Our various forms of participation in the act of creation continue to enhance our lives, making the world more marvelous, a blessing to all who partake in its beauty.

Creativity is a fascinating thing. It takes on a magical quality when you release your inner fears and let love for life and everything else guide your heart. Even when it seems like you're taking risks, you should make it the only tune you listen to, striving for perfection in every possible way, despite the pressures surrounding you. Stay loyal to the gift you've been granted; cherish it genuinely because it defines who you are. While there are distractions that can lead you astray, genuine love for your talents is designed to bring out the best in both you and your pursuits.

Live your life with the understanding that it's the only thing that can shield you from the challenges the world throws at you, eager to consume your spirit and your knowledge of this existence. Ultimately, you can attain a serene existence, using your unique perspective to shed light on our shared human experience. Everything you grasp about the world we inhabit can be acknowledged and utilized to contribute positively to our planet.

The knowledge that transforms into reality within us possesses the power to heal essential aspects of humanity. Strive to transcend ordinary existence, so that others may find inspiration within you, setting you apart by constantly pushing your boundaries.

As you push yourself, holding onto the foundations of our lives, you become profoundly shaped by a distinctive form of comprehension that is rarely encountered in the world. You evolve into a reflection of a high-quality life and knowledge, something we all carry within us, albeit often locked away in the depths of our thoughts, accessible only through our affection for particular aspects of reality. It's the love we hold for certain facets of this world that unlocks the gates hidden deep within us.

Without dedication, you might stay unaware and miss the path meant for you. We all have a part of ourselves that's locked away, and only genuine love can unlock those hidden doors. With determination, we can make that place our home, and we won't need to force ourselves anymore. Don't be like those who can't see the way and stick to others' beliefs. Keep faith at the center of everything you do.

Sometimes, it can be easy or tough to lose faith, which is crucial, and it guides our lives. We lose control of who we are, turning away from our core until we're vulnerable. True love is the force that fuels our existence. Everything can seem meaningless, leaving us with nothing to live for. But love keeps everything alive and restores our dignity, no matter what goes wrong.

Pressure can destroy what you've known, but genuine commitment can preserve your essence, even when it feels like everything is falling apart. So, when you live your dream, connect it deep within your soul, where you genuinely love, not just crave life and everything else. True love for the world is a constant source of life and wisdom. When the path forward gets hazy, it becomes the energy that brings us back to reality, making us human once more. It serves as a reminder not to overlook but to deeply consider it.

Genuine devotion to everything that defines us is a rare and valuable achievement. Once we attain it, we should hold onto it because it brings out our best qualities. Sometimes, you might consider leaving love or talent behind, which can be disappointing. You may have the determination to continue, but lack the energy to make it a reality. It's when you combine commitment and talent that you start to see your true potential unfold. This is followed by the daily sacrifices necessary for our progress and happiness.

We let go of things that no longer serve us and embrace a new way of life, which becomes an integral part of our existence. Discover your strengths and nurture your talents in areas that matter to you in this world. Be willing to sacrifice to become what you aspire to be. Building your dreams on a foundation of care and understanding is crucial, as so much of what we need is built upon it.

The love that becomes the center of our lives brings a deep satisfaction that makes us feel present and accomplished. Regardless of how much we give, it never seems enough to fully grasp our destiny. True love in our hearts allows us to hold onto our lives and find contentment in who we are. Whether or not we've reached our ultimate destiny, something can satisfy us, addressing the question of how we want to make an impact with the knowledge we possess.

Maybe there wasn't a better path to choose, and you might wonder what the ideal route is. Regardless of the message you aim to convey about yourself, there's our own self-awareness, which holds significant importance to you alone. As life progresses to a certain stage, it becomes the foremost priority, the very essence you wish to witness materialize. It validates the sense of pride dwelling within us, stemming from the determination not to yield. It boils down to your unwavering resolve to bring your desires to fruition and find contentment in all things.

In this vast world, amidst the myriad experiences it offers, a select few will reaffirm your inherent worth. Among these, true love, experienced in the way you envisioned loving and being loved, and life lived in accordance with your ideals, emerge as pivotal. This prompts introspection: What does it signify to you personally when your envisioned ideals manifest into reality, when you witness the transformation unfolding through your comprehension?

If you can reintegrate your understanding into the fabric of life, you will have surpassed the requisite and attainable. Embarking on the journey of life as you envisage it is no simple task, but upon reaching your destination, the world will acknowledge your efforts. This is the type of accomplishment that tends to define us and grant us the best that life has to offer, all because we possess this distinctive gift. You've mastered something exceedingly rare in our existence, carving a means to connect with humanity. Breaking through to your own unique level isn't an everyday occurrence, but occasionally, you can become someone recognized and comprehended for what you genuinely represent.

The people who become a part of your life can repay you for the efforts you've put into what you love to create. Love brings us together at the center of creativity and infuses life into it. Love magnifies our efforts and broadens our creative horizons. There's so much happiness to be found in this, but often we overlook it, failing to realize its importance in our lives. However, you've witnessed how it works and the positive outcomes it can bring when treated with care.

It's challenging to reach your destiny all alone, and this is where you'll encounter the most struggles. The battle can be quite consuming and can even affect you deeply. All the efforts we extend to the world out there require someone to receive them, and love is the means by which we continually practice the art of living and acceptance. True love embraces us daily for who we are, and it's the reward we receive for all the effort we put out into the world. Essentially, what we consistently practice becomes our reality, and the daily exchange of giving and receiving becomes our world.

So, without reservation, consider permanently surrendering yourself to love, for you will need it. Why not open your heart now and offer all that you are right where you are? Witness how love becomes the driving force behind everything you do. Without love, much of what we are and do lacks a significant purpose to serve. It's not as if the world insists that you can't be content with yourself without that tender love in your heart; you can, but you won't feel complete without it.

If circumstances become challenging and there's no alternative, you must fully commit yourself. Although it may sometimes be challenging to summon this level of dedication, you can start with modest beginnings. This is particularly relevant in today's demanding world, where our expectations continually rise, and we strive to achieve the extraordinary. Dedication is something accessible to all of us, even if it seems difficult to attain. You just need to look within yourself.

At times, the most precious qualities are concealed within us, waiting to be uncovered, regardless of the conventional notions that life is predictable. Our deepest desires may be hidden, but within you, as you are, there exists the potential to discover someone who can bring out the best in you.

You may have a grasp of your current situation, but mistakenly believe that it's sufficient for the long haul. Unfortunately, this assumption can betray you, leading to profound disappointment and a struggle to rediscover your true self. If you continue down this path, you may squander numerous opportunities for happiness and self-discovery. Genuine love is a precious and elusive treasure. Opportunities to pursue happiness and self-awareness are limited, and if you miss them, love may not wait for you to decide what you truly desire.

Many changes will occur in how you used to understand things, and it can be quite sorrowful when you realize that certain actions are irreversible. Time has passed, and you cannot compensate for it. It's disheartening when you find yourself in a lower position due to ignoring obvious issues. Why do we neglect caring like that, allowing significant opportunities to slip away without realizing what truly matters in our lives? Sometimes, it's not just about choosing who to give your heart to; it's about dedicating yourself to achieving your desires in this world.

However, to succeed, you must be competitive and strategic, and this isn't something that comes easily. Discovering that inner strength and passion can't be forced through love. In some cases, love represents a point of acceptance where people can easily connect with our actions. You effortlessly blend in with their comfort zone. Yet, there's a profound love for what you do that becomes magical, as it unlocks the doors to endless possibilities.

You begin to grasp the essence of life, as beyond your knowledge, it's the deepest part of yourself you can offer. Even when obstacles attempt to hold you back, having this love makes you resilient, guiding you towards a brighter path. It's our lack of commitment that often hinders contentment in our lives.

Love is when you release your inhibitions and evolve into a new, improved version of yourself. Amidst the common traits found in humans, you choose something unique and essential for our lives. You learn to embrace this understanding as an inherent part of your being, and the more you infuse life with this feeling, the more doors to your deepest desires swing open. So, when true love seems elusive, you can ask yourself: do you turn away forever, or do you cultivate this feeling within yourself, knowing it's enough for all your desires?

What if you've given generously to your desires, and there's nothing left to offer to the available opportunities? You might be left pondering life's questions and constantly reflecting on the world you once knew, now seemingly devoured by a strong desire for worldly possessions. Even though we all believe we deserve something pure for ourselves, it can be taken away, becoming a distant memory. Understanding may become elusive, and the dedication you longed for may seem out of reach.

Before you voice your concerns about the persistent absence of love or repeatedly question how it vanished from your life, consider how it went awry. Could it be due to a lack of motivation in discovering the best aspects of our lives? Sometimes, we view situations as if there will always be a second chance to make things right. However, opportunities to correct our mistakes may be scarce, but remember, you had good intentions. The time you spend complaining may represent a missed opportunity because you had a deep commitment to so much in this world.

You couldn't always be available for every aspect of life. Sometimes, you needed to go out and explore, discover yourself, and search for something or someone to wholeheartedly devote your attention to; otherwise, life might

60

seem devoid of purpose. Now that you've found a deep appreciation for the world and a special someone who stands by your side, everything you hold dear refuses to simply align and make sense. You may feel like you're battling against the current of life, as if committing to someone isn't sufficient to encompass all your cares.

You can sit back and contemplate the world you've grown to cherish, yet there was a time when we found joy in the simple ideas we wholeheartedly embraced. It's disheartening that if the gates to love remain closed, you know you're not succeeding. True success means being welcomed back into the embrace of humanity, in a universe that adores not only you but also approves of your every facet, swinging wide the doors of life to reveal your place in it.

The prospect of failing to discover where you belong or having your ideas go unnoticed feels more like a descent into madness than a mere struggle to find your niche. You might seem like a person desperately clinging to sanity in the realm of creativity. It's the result of losing your foothold in this platform of imagination. Yet, now that you've become lost within the realm of art, how would you categorize that experience? You yearned for clarity so intensely, believing that, deep down, everything was fine. However, you can't find contentment in the lives of others.

Chapter Six

Amazed

Don't find yourself stuck in predictable situations and hope for something worthwhile at the end of the day. You can't predict what life has in store for you. Sometimes, everything might seem like it's working against you, even time itself. So instead of not understanding your goals, put in efforts that will amaze everyone.

Here's the thing: knowing something is one thing, and being talented is another. Talent is a unique quality in a person. It's when you view life differently and possess the potential to astonish the world. When you reach the end, you'll realize that you are your greatest asset. You'll understand that not many people care about your success – the only one who truly cares about your well-being is yourself. Throughout your life, that's what you can rely on, the one thing that can relieve the pressures you face.

In life, you'll encounter challenges, and many things may try to hold you back from achieving your true desires. That's because the world isn't designed to make things easy for anyone. We're all in this together, pulling the same weight, and comfort is hard to come by.

You need to make your actions count, regardless of your knowledge. Don't waste your life waiting in line for something uncertain. Don't invest your time in paths that don't lead to your growth, as no amount of time can fix that lack of progress.

Talent is an essential tool that you must recognize within yourself. It's different from merely loving something; it's about finding your unique place to shine. So, how can you make it work? It's crucial to value your time because spending too long pondering an idea without progress can lead to disappointment. Instead of moving forward, you may end up with nothing to show for your efforts.

When you take things seriously, you unlock deeper levels of understanding and see the value of your efforts materialize. Don't become complacent; pursue what truly matters to you. If something seems important from a distance, it remains crucial up close. Remember, success often depends on your mindset. Always keep in mind that embarking on a journey to understand something better is a step in the right direction.

You've just set off a process that aims to make humans weaker with each passing day. Imagine our world as having various levels of existence, some straightforward and others more challenging. On the simpler levels, people lead typical lives and engage in everyday activities. They wake up each morning and perform routine, practical tasks, and in this way, their lives maintain a straightforward simplicity throughout their existence.

On the solid foundation, people pursue their desires freely, finding satisfaction in activities driven by their personal interests. This autonomy is what adds complexity to the situation. We're driven by our own desires, and nobody else can assist us in achieving them. It feels wrong for others to meddle in our pursuits, for these endeavors are sources of personal joy.

No one truly cares about your wishes, and as such, no one is responsible for safeguarding your best interests. You must take diligent care of yourself. It's crucial not to adopt a self-limiting mindset that relies on others for strength. Instead, you should be self-motivated, fully aware of your actions, and how to derive benefits from them.

When you possess talent, you wield a powerful tool capable of overcoming seemingly insurmountable obstacles. Confidence in your abilities allows you to navigate challenging terrain with ease. Through your thoughts, you can connect with others, even though realizing many of our thoughts can be difficult without artistic discipline.

Lacking the courage to see the world as it truly exists can lead to self-imposed limitations. It's essential to recognize that you've come a long way to reach your current point, and failing to grasp the bigger picture can hinder your progress. We must focus on self-improvement, gaining a clear understanding of our actions, and avoiding a lifetime of self-imposed setbacks.

When we try something new for the first time, we often feel uncertain. However, it's essential to have faith that when embarking on a journey aligned with our passions, help will be available. This assistance will come when we've done our part and shown ourselves to be unique and valuable. Therefore, it's crucial to work diligently and understand that we are like a product to others. We must maintain high quality to gain recognition.

In life, obstacles may temporarily block our path, but we should equip ourselves to impress the world. When an opportunity arises, we should seize it wisely. If this is the only life we know, we shouldn't be discouraged by others. Remember that people possess diverse skills and abilities. Some are content with being ordinary, while others maximize every opportunity.

Never forget what initially inspired you to pursue your current path. Challenges are inevitable, and some may seem discouraging. However, realize that they are just small parts of the life you aspire to live. We all have different goals in this journey.

Your success depends on your knowledge and the territory you create with it. The more you understand, the better you can connect with people worldwide. Your life starts with a certain level of understanding, and you'll encounter various individuals who motivate you in different ways. Always strive to build trust in your unique way of thinking.

Do not allow the place where you were born to restrict your opportunities, especially if you are not fully confident in your endeavors. Look beyond your current circumstances and strive to expand your knowledge. Your natural abilities will always be there to reward your efforts. Keep in mind that it's important to appeal to various types of people, so work on self-improvement, knowing that the entire world is your stage.

If you fail to do what is expected of you, you will limit your potential because you won't effectively communicate with the world. Interact with others in a way that everyone can understand you, utilizing your unique talents.

Although challenges may arise as you pursue your goals, proper preparation will help you understand people better. Sometimes, when you reach out to people, you might attract the wrong audience, but you're never completely off the mark. As you define your identity, you'll discover who appreciates your work and who your intended audience is.

Gain a clear understanding of your identity, goals, and desired outcomes. You have control over everything you work on. See yourself as a product shaped by your understanding and ask yourself: Who am I? Who appreciates my work, and how do people react to it?

While you may not always excel at delivering an engaging message that resonates with everyone, you can create content in a language that is understood by a global audience. This common language is often the first step in connecting with people and gaining their attention. Avoid narrow-mindedness by staying informed about the evolving world and finding ways to make your message accessible to all.

Show the world your brilliance and deep understanding of how things are created and how you define yourself and your perspective. If you fail to grasp the universe's essence, you risk losing relevance in our world and its core values. So, establish your comprehension and find where you can contribute meaningfully. If you're eager and committed to personal growth, you'll progress and become the person you've always envisioned. No one can hinder you or quash your dreams. Art and creativity are integral to our identity, something we must cherish in our lives.

When you view your surroundings differently, it becomes a crucial part of conveying your unique perspective. You inhabit your own creation; what can you do to impact the lives of those around you? Go beyond expectations, offering a unique contribution driven by your understanding, a trait that defines us as humans. Shaping the world's affection toward you is your responsibility, recognizing your worth as you comprehend the world.

The key to fulfilling your deepest desires is that it doesn't matter who you are or where you come from – that's the beauty of talent, realizing that a new world constantly emerges. So, only excellence and dedication in your work will leave a lasting mark, bearing a special quality that shines eternally. With exceptional talent, everything can pause to make way for your star, and no one can take that away from you. No reputation can hinder you when it's your time to share your thoughts.

Your life is like a strong fortress that you build with the knowledge and understanding you gain from the world. For a while, you'll be at the center of attention, and nothing can disrupt the flow of your life. Your talents are powerful tools that speak volumes about who you are. They can reshape our understanding of things and pave the way for your unique contributions. You can't be underestimated; you mark the beginning of something significant in this world. You have the potential to alter history and redefine the way we perceive life.

Don't miss out on the greatest adventure of human existence—the story and the central theme of everything that defines us as humans. It's the very reason we're here, our greatest achievement in life. However, sometimes, we miss the point and inadvertently convey the wrong message about something so valuable and integral to our way of life. Always remember your purpose in the world—to entertain, excite, and motivate. Success is vital, as it becomes the cornerstone of the attention we seek. What you aim to achieve says a lot, and for people to understand your work, you must present it from a unique angle and stay true to your vision.

When navigating the path where knowledge about life is invaluable, be the person who embodies this wisdom. Though you may occasionally lose your way in the depths of your journey, your commitment to excellence and honesty will guide you back. While we aren't born with this knowledge, we can recognize when something isn't serving its purpose. Sometimes, you might think you're doing something exceptionally well when, in reality, you're not. However, the truth is always evident, and when you reach your best, you'll feel yourself ascending to a higher level of understanding.

When you're exploring the world with the power of knowledge, you may not discover your true self until you reach a point where you excel in your chosen path. This transformation often happens when you embark on journeys of discovery and embrace new experiences in life. Letting go of the familiar can be one of the most profound sacrifices we make, but it's essential to recognize that when something isn't going as planned, it's time to explore alternative approaches. While talent is undoubtedly valuable and stands out, sometimes we generate brilliant ideas without knowing how to bring them to fruition.

To truly persevere, you must have unwavering faith in yourself, to the extent that you're willing to risk it all for your goals. Along this journey, we accumulate valuable knowledge and insights, gradually evolving into our true selves. We don't start with all the wisdom we need; instead, we begin at a stage where our efforts reflect the early days of our life's journey. Only through relentless hard work and dedication can we progress from this initial stage to the more advanced phases of life.

We develop qualities over time through dedication and effort, even if we aren't born with them. These qualities become integral to our identity and are aspects we genuinely appreciate about ourselves. By persistently pushing ourselves, we achieve success in these areas. Deep down, we all have the potential for greatness, and if you can't recognize that amazing person within you, you'll struggle to meet the expectations placed upon you, regardless of how inadequate you may feel.

There's a purpose meant for each of us, and you can discover it when you commit yourself to a noble cause that brings out the best in us as human beings. We all possess unique attributes to offer, and while you may not always be at your peak, there are moments and phases where your brilliance will shine. When the world opens doors for you to showcase your capabilities, that's when it becomes a defining moment of our humanity.

Don't let that time in your life slip away; utilize it wisely to nurture your knowledge and talents. This phase is immensely significant in shaping who we are, and it's interwoven into our life journey. As you grow and mature in a particular direction, you are molded by your understanding of creativity. Everyone faces moments of uncertainty about their aspirations, and it can be challenging when the world doesn't yet grasp your essence and values.

The more you wholeheartedly embrace creativity, the more you evolve into a person capable of filling a unique space that no one else can occupy. You might feel alone in experiencing this phase of life, but many have embarked on a similar journey, gradually improving with time. It's the ongoing commitment to a pursuit that helps us realize where our efforts truly belong. With time, we grow, acknowledging that we won't remain stagnant forever.

Every time you put in effort, you embark on a journey through life, and you develop as you pursue your goals. Life unfolds in stages, and within these stages, you'll discover opportunities to apply your knowledge effectively. As you progress through each stage, you'll reach a point where you become the center of attention, receiving the recognition and respect you deserve.

Even as time marches on, it will always bring something valuable into your life.

Throughout your existence, you'll savor the fruits of the world's contributions to your journey. You won't remain in obscurity forever; when your moment arrives, seize it and relish the human experience. Make room for others who also have something meaningful to share with the world, knowing that your time was just a chapter in history.

Remember that others paved the way for you, and you now comprehend that we are neither the first nor the last. We must acknowledge that others possess similar talents for creation. While you, on the other hand, have had your moments of acceptance by the world. Understand that you can never revert to the person you once were, and whether new or old, you may step aside at times to make space for newcomers. Yet, deep within, you'll always hold a special place in people's hearts, representing a unique chapter in their lives that no one can replace.

If you've selected something significant to represent in people's lives, you may need to allow others to shine too. However, hold onto the theme that's become yours due to your determination. Even when the world can or cannot talk freely about things, we still cling to what truly belongs to us. This is because what we stand for reveals a lot about who we are as individuals. It's not just for a single day but for the entirety of our lives. This is what we'll be remembered for, and it's what remains in people's hearts even after we're gone.

Right now, all we have is today and tomorrow while we're still alive. After we've passed away, nobody really cares about who we were. However, if we stood for something unique, it's our legacy that will endure through time. So, don't hesitate to express what you've learned about life. Anything genuine you have to share with the world will find a place in someone's heart.

Do you possess knowledge or understanding that's truly worth sharing with the world? Something that will define you for the rest of your life? Our actions and what we understand about creation speak volumes about us. So, convey your thoughts and ideas through your work. Reach out to countless people and leave behind a legacy of knowledge and a life story that won't fade from memory. We aren't defined solely by our origins; sometimes, we set aside our past and choose something special for our lives. When the time comes to decide what's truly worthy of who you are, follow the path that leads to your inner self, which is the essence of your being.

Don't just select something because it pleases you or others for a short while. Incorporate all the good qualities of life, like caring, and understand that eventually, you'll have to answer for your choices. So, if you were merely delighted to focus on a particular aspect of life without a sincere foundation in human hearts and souls, time will pass, and you might lose significance due to what you aim to represent about people. From the moment you get a chance to showcase your creativity, it becomes a timeless moment that will endure forever.

For a brief moment, it shouldn't only be about you; people desire to feel welcome in your life. It should encompass so much more. When you've deeply considered who you are and where you fit into people's lives, then regardless of the challenges life throws at you, you'll always make progress. This happens because you've chosen something genuine and worth sharing with the world. When you step out into the world equipped with your knowledge and understanding, your wisdom about life will radiate throughout the universe.

People may underestimate your true potential, but when you've chosen a noble cause, you'll be astonished by your capacity for creation. The toughest part is always at the start, where you must declare your intentions. After selecting your path, you embark on a journey that leads to your desired destination. Along the way, you gather a wealth of knowledge, but it's the attitude from deep within your heart that unlocks doors to endless possibilities.

Even in the theme we've chosen for ourselves, you'll have the opportunity to truly understand its significance, and people will witness what you hold close to your heart. There will come a time when everything you've embraced as part of your knowledge will be highlighted, and it must strongly reflect your values for everyone to see who you are. Think about what it would be like if you had been self-centered. Humanity would discover aspects of your character that may not be admirable.

The world has many common aspects, and this is something you'll come to realize in the end. So, when you want to communicate with the world, approach them with something that is relatable to all of us as humans. Many will find your theme accommodating. When you step into the spotlight, they will easily feel a connection with everything you represent, even if not everyone can fully relate to your life. However, even after your time has passed, they will continue to sense your presence, not merely as a fleeting figure but as a lasting influence.

This area of knowledge was once considered a vital part of people's lives. In the end, it surprised many when they saw how deeply you cared. Despite our individual efforts, we all share a commonality as human beings, serving as our point of connection with the broader world. This is what truly reveals your character, your place in the world, and your understanding of it.

Imagine if you find it challenging to grasp something that's common among us humans. You realize that you're struggling to meet the most basic requirements for being understood by everyone. You should aim to approach things in a way that makes people easily connect with whatever you're involved in.

Learn to communicate with fellow human beings by drawing on your understanding of life, your knowledge of the world we inhabit, and your ability to help others improve their circumstances. While we may not possess all-encompassing talent and knowledge, we can certainly strive to be sufficiently knowledgeable and attentive to the well-being of others. Recognize that this will ultimately yield a significant impact and empower individuals to manage their lives effectively. To achieve this, you must commit yourself wholeheartedly to the role you wish to embody, ensuring that what you offer to the world aligns with what you expect in return.

Provide them with knowledge to conquer their fears, and in return, they will offer you the same to overcome your personal challenges. There exists within each and every one of us a profound commonality—a shared human experience that bridges the gap between our individuality and diverse backgrounds. You must have undergone a significant journey of personal growth, shaped by your unique perspective.

If your purpose is to excite and entertain, then do so with enthusiasm and captivating content. If your mission is to educate and motivate, then be informative and inspirational, ensuring people derive satisfaction from engaging with you. Value people's time, and derive contentment from your ability to excel in these endeavors. If you possess the skills, don't hesitate to deploy them, understanding that your efforts will resonate deeply within people's hearts, filling them with gratitude and joy.

You've provided people with what they needed based on your knowledge. If you hadn't done this for them, you might have spent your whole life feeling like you didn't have a clear purpose. Imagine being lost in your own world. We grow through our interactions, and consider the satisfaction that comes from giving people what they desire and growing alongside them.

Dedication should reside at the core of your heart so that, at some point, you can grasp how to fulfill people's wishes and find fulfillment for yourself. You dedicated your life to satisfying human desires, and that can be your greatest reward for all your efforts. You could have been critical of yourself and acted as your own judge when you recognized your mistakes. But now, you understand what you're doing, even though it's clear that we can be our own worst enemies. Nevertheless, you must acknowledge your accomplishments because, for the first time, you know you've done things correctly and for all the right reasons.

We aren't born with innate knowledge. Although we enter this uncomplicated world, you could have succeeded even in the most challenging environments known to humankind. If obstacles have stood in your way from the beginning, then you have fulfilled your destiny. Sometimes, people can keep going in circles without understanding what's making life difficult for them.

You might often find yourself pondering why your life seems confusing, and why you often stumble and face setbacks while pursuing your goals. Nevertheless, the world continuously beckons us to explore our lives because we each have a unique purpose. It's important to remember that this journey isn't without effort; you've likely faced moments of uncertainty and had to demonstrate your unwavering dedication to your passions or understanding of the universe to achieve a sense of freedom.

Sometimes, you might question why your focus doesn't align with the reality others experience. However, it's essential to recognize that our perspectives are molded by our individual life experiences. Occasionally, it's your own experiences that can hinder your progress, leaving you puzzled about what's amiss in your life. You may have lost interest in aspects of life that once seemed common and essential to people, yet you yearn for things to regain their significance.

In the distant future, many pieces of the puzzle will come together, and life will start to make more sense. It's vital to cherish love and strive for improvement in the present moment.

Chapter Seven

The Will or the Way

Even when things are tough, you have to make choices that are best for you. It's not just about money, love, or family; it's about finding your purpose. In the midst of all the chaos, you are the most important person. You must do your part to make things happen, even if there are times when you lack motivation.

We strive to keep moving forward, but sometimes our efforts fall short of our goals. We all want to feel comfortable, but true comfort may only come once we've reached our destination. It might not always feel comfortable along the way, but it's necessary for progress and achieving your goals.

Sometimes you may doubt your abilities, but that's when you need to expand your horizons. It can be frustrating when you can't see the path ahead, but keep pushing yourself. Your current goal might seem challenging, but don't settle until everything aligns the way you want it to.

Life can be tough, but give it your all. With determination, you can reach the next level of what you're seeking in this world.

Don't ever think that achieving your dreams is impossible. The possibility is always there; you just need to give it your all – your heart, mind, and soul.

Sometimes, you might find yourself stuck at a certain point, with a clear vision but lacking the know-how. Not everything you need is within easy reach. Some people only have the desire and willpower to view the world with a positive attitude and make a positive impact.

You might face obstacles and challenges, but these are what propel you forward. Achieving your dreams brings a deep sense of satisfaction to your life. It's important to have goals that are meaningful and challenging. These goals give your life purpose and make it exciting.

Life wouldn't be worth living if there were no goals to strive for. Your existence gains meaning when you have important goals to pursue. Even though you may not always see the path clearly, having goals is the foundation of a meaningful life. Use them as your starting point for progress and growth. This can make the journey of creation and self-discovery exciting.

Having a goal to dedicate your efforts to is one of the best reasons to live. It gives your life purpose and fulfillment. While there may be moments when the way forward seems unclear, remember that barriers can be overcome. Breaking down these walls allows you to travel toward your goals and watch your dreams become a reality. This process makes you a better person, and deep down, we all need a reason to shine like stars.

When you have a purpose that seems incredibly challenging to attain, you can rise above your comfort zone through faith and unwavering belief. Often, we find ourselves navigating the complex path of existence, driven by our desire to acquire more. This journey may seem bewildering, but deep down, you know it's what you truly desire. The persistent difficulty of pursuing your heart's desire lingers in your soul. You chase after something you genuinely need, even as questions about why you persist arise.

Along this path, we learn many valuable lessons, yet it often feels like we lack the precise knowledge required to achieve our true aspirations. It may be exceedingly challenging, but how can you abandon something you've envisioned and holds a place in your heart?

No matter how daunting the journey, if you maintain your belief, you will be granted the opportunity to become everything you deserve. You can attain all you've ever desired, even when it occasionally feels like you're conjuring fantasies that may never materialize. Despite time's reluctance to reveal your dreams, you must persist in your belief and hope for the best.

Whether you feel bound or not, there comes a point when our goals become an integral part of our identity. Our minds are shaped by these objectives, ultimately influencing the people we become and our contribution to the world.

The role we have in people's lives is determined by the kind of people we choose to be. When you view the world through the lens of an idea you value and understand, your responses are shaped by that perspective. When you've truly seen the world and can't look away, no one can blind you or obscure your vision. Once you've witnessed something, it becomes a permanent part of you, and a part of you may always carry the weight of that experience.

So, how do you cope with unfulfilled dreams, knowing that a part of you longs for normalcy and a desire to see the world as a better place? You may wish for peace, regardless of your origins. Our dreams can become the most significant aspect of our lives, and turning them into reality can be a costly endeavor.

Even love, at times, can be elusive, requiring a determined effort to make it a reality. In the process, we may lose parts of ourselves, and the journey can feel like losing our way. We continue to live, with the sole aim of healing the scars left by unfulfilled desires, which can affect every facet of our being.

We are human because we yearn for achievement and personal growth. We become better by pursuing our objectives. However, when we're not making progress toward our goals or parts of us remain unfulfilled, it can be disorienting, leaving us without a clear path forward. Without someone to care for us, true happiness can feel elusive, especially when love remains intangible. In such times, we are merely humans, navigating life with faith, holding onto whatever semblance of existence we can find.

While recognizing that this may not fully reflect your true self, a portion of your life as a star remains unrealized, and you cannot firmly grasp onto anyone or anything. Instead, you must cultivate self-reliance and place your trust in your own abilities to comprehend and be confident in your actions. Even though you may harbor fears of potential failure, you persist in your journey, and that's precisely why achieving your goals holds such significant value. Many sacrifices have been made to bring this dream to fruition.

So, how can you justify your efforts when it seems like you're working in vain? Understand that you must endure by having faith and moving forward. Only when you reach your objective will your hard work be vindicated. Remember, it's not merely about dreaming; it's about achieving your dreams in the end.

Now, the spotlight is on you. Seize this golden opportunity, the greatest chance of your lifetime. Make history, impact the world, and earn the respect you deserve. There's no greater purpose in life than this. If you possess the will, you'll find the way to surpass countless others who have come before you. Dedicate yourself wholeheartedly and firmly believe that this pursuit is the most meaningful aspect of your entire existence, surpassing all else.

The lifestyle you've yearned for, once deemed impossible, has evolved alongside you. Now, it's within your grasp. Despite its initial challenges, it has become attainable and can materialize effortlessly.

Many times, it may seem like achieving our dreams is impossible because of our upbringing, and many things are beyond our abilities. These things are not part of our formal education; instead, we learn through our determination to become the best versions of ourselves. Even though life may have moved forward without us, our understanding alone can help us reach our goals. It's important to learn how to be self-reliant and watch yourself thrive through your own knowledge. Realize how significant you are to everything you aspire to achieve.

Try to grow alongside your pursuits, or else you may lose value in everything around you. Love is a precious gift that we cannot give to ourselves, and as humans, we need someone special to love us. Therefore, work diligently to provide love and kindness to those who need it, and in return, you will also receive the warmth and affection that only one individual can offer. This acceptance comes when you strive to understand, even though it may be intimidating.

At times, it may feel like we no longer matter or that we're not meeting society's expectations. During these moments, it's essential to remember that you're not lost; you've experienced moments of greatness that prove you are capable of understanding your path. You've been focused on your aspirations, but how you handle being recognized is a separate matter. You can gain fame for your talents and expertise, becoming renowned for what you excel at.

Understand the importance of putting in hard work and continually improving yourself to meet the expectations of others and the standards set for creation. Each day, as you put in more effort, you move closer to gaining a better understanding. Remember, we aren't born with this knowledge; we acquire it through our efforts. The more you engage in your activities, the more skilled you become, eventually reaching the level where you're needed. Don't blame humanity for the changes you've had to undergo or the intelligence you've had to gain; much of it comes at a cost.

Many sacrifices must be made, and some may be hard to comprehend. You might have to endure loneliness and the feeling of being rejected by everything around you. It may seem like people can sense your unease and choose not to be a part of it. Without meeting these requirements, your life may not progress to a deeper level of understanding. You can't rely on the hope that your life will improve solely by acquiring knowledge. However, when you become knowledgeable, it can feel like a heavy burden has been lifted, making it easier to achieve your goals.

It all depends on your commitment to being human and dedicating yourself to your endeavors. This dedication is what allows you to achieve anything. It's when you've given your all and there's no turning back. You commit yourself completely to something, even if you don't succeed immediately. Part of you always strives towards your creative goals. As a result, everything in your daily life aligns more effortlessly with your desires. Deep down, you continue doing what's expected of you, even when you feel like giving up at times.

Embrace the precious gift that you have received, even when life feels routine and ordinary. Commit to your responsibilities wholeheartedly and fulfill the purpose within your heart. Seek to connect with others and offer the love they need. We all carry profound emotions within us, and to remember our humanity, we must learn to both love and be loved. Share a part of your true self and be open to acceptance from others. There is always someone out there in search of genuine affection, just as you long to be cared for. Don't hesitate; express your true essence.

Patience isn't merely waiting; it's about taking proactive steps and dedicating yourself to love while also pursuing your goals. Sometimes, it's essential to prioritize relationships even in challenging circumstances. Allocate space in your life to care for someone because this is how we overcome difficulties and grow as individuals. Keep your heart strong, understanding that you can progress steadily, rather than trying to do everything at once. Take gradual steps toward your destined place, and in doing so, you may find deeper meaning along the way.

Prepare yourself for all challenges because many things can test your abilities to the fullest, evaluating whether you truly comprehend your actions. If you genuinely embody your professed qualities, you must grasp the potential impact of the durations of your projects and the potential harm they could inflict. Do you align with the timeframes these endeavors demand? Moreover, are you attentive to the repercussions of your work, especially concerning how it influences the ever-changing world we inhabit? Are you focused on the transient nature of life's passage or the detrimental effects it may have on our quality of life? If you indeed possess enduring strength, regardless of the protracted nature of endeavors, they cannot thwart your chances of success; rather, they fortify your resilience.

Therefore, direct your attention comprehensively in this manner, recognizing your pursuit of a high-quality lifestyle capable of withstanding any adversity to find your rightful place. To achieve this, you must connect with fellow human beings, conveying your sentiments about various matters and consistently delivering value through your endeavors. You must fulfill your responsibilities, adapting as necessary to confront any obstacles. In doing so, you will uncover your true worth and realize that it warrants the recognition and acclaim you desire. Our desires from the realm of creation are extensive, but it's crucial to reflect on whether we genuinely merit the costs involved. Furthermore, attaining maturity need not catch you unawares; seize the prime opportunity to exert effort and evolve alongside life's challenges.

t some point in your journey, ensure that you muster great courage to confront the future armed with knowledge. Strive to attain profound wisdom and grasp the art of altering your fate, even if it appears daunting and feels like surrendering to uncertainty. Dedicate yourself to becoming the best version of yourself, and you will eventually witness opportunities materializing. Embrace the essence of who you are and your passions, for you have consciously chosen this path to safeguard your inner self. Just as we realize our potential, we become like stars on the horizon, for it becomes our only conceivable path in life. Remember, it's crucial not to yield prematurely or arrive late.

How can you justify relinquishing your current identity in pursuit of a fulfilling life? Whether you embark on this transformation early or start paying heed to your deepest passions, the outcome remains unchanged. The truth is, if this is destined to be your sole path, you must be willing to sacrifice everything else to find meaning, even if it seems too early to commit to it exclusively. What if you don't succeed and have already given your all, as if the future had guaranteed something more? What if your efforts end in failure, leaving you with nothing else to live for, and your entire journey appears ruined? Conversely, if you delay until it's almost too late, what if your dedication never truly makes sense, and you are left with little humanity to hold onto?

On both occasions, it often feels like we've already taken quite significant risks, and you may wonder if it's worth risking your life for something you're uncertain about. Pledging your life to an uncertain outcome can make you question if the chances we're taking are truly worth the sacrifices we're making, and if our hopeful vision of the future will materialize. Without doubting your own abilities and with a clear sense of purpose, you must act. Regardless of how long it may take, it's crucial to keep moving forward because life doesn't wait for anyone.

Undoubtedly, every decision carries weight, and the prospect of taking risks can be daunting. Choosing to forsake love, security, and stability to venture down a challenging path raises uncertainties about the outcome. We grapple with the possibility that the future might offer nothing in return, leaving us with fewer accomplishments and potentially losing our core values. At the end of the day, is it worth taking these extraordinary risks? When you embark on this journey, nothing else seems to matter.

Do we always get exactly what we're searching for at the end of the day, or do we sometimes feel disappointed when we realize that we can't have everything we desire? It's important to reflect on our journey and whether we're taking too many risks to achieve success. Are we required to commit wholeheartedly to guarantee success, or are some of us born destined for success, regardless of when or how we pursue it? Sometimes, we fear having to let go of our past selves in order to reach for the stars. We must be willing to let go of our old selves to become the people meant for greater things, even though this path is unknown to us. The only option is to persevere.

If you still have multiple options, it's possible you haven't yet reached your ultimate destination. When you've truly arrived at your destination, all you have left is your life as a star. Having choices can be a distraction on your path to greatness and becoming the person you aspire to be. It can be challenging for us to accept our current state when we compare it to our ideal selves. This is when we should consider our options in light of our goals and intended purpose. Did we prepare adequately for all aspects of life, or did we focus solely on a glamorous star-like lifestyle?

Why didn't we acquire a broad range of skills and knowledge to ensure success in any direction we choose? Having multiple skills can provide alternative options when one path falters. Unfortunately, we often find ourselves with only one true calling: to be a dedicated individual who nurtures their unique talent, a gift that doesn't come easily. We must use it wisely, work diligently, and commit our entire being to it. Success means giving everything we are and having nothing left, fully embracing our purpose without distraction. Belief in ourselves is paramount; nothing else truly matters. The path we've chosen is a personal one, and recognizing it as our only chance to make a difference is key.

It seems like we're taking a big risk, but it might actually help us deal with the uncertainties we usually face. You must be confident in your actions; that's no excuse to avoid doing what's expected of you. You commit to this life, knowing it's your true calling. You become the person you need to be, no matter the cost of success. You persist in your chosen path and ensure you're not chasing unrealistic dreams deep within your mind. This path is your chosen one among numerous possibilities. Despite occasional feelings of being stuck, you persevere. How do you cope during those times when you can't find your way?

It's a tough world, and when you decide to become something, you must be certain it's what you truly desire. Yet, we're required to be so much more, but we're afraid to fully commit. We only reveal a fraction of ourselves to maintain other options, even though it might be more comfortable to conform. However, this isn't the life we were meant to lead. Embracing this lifestyle means you've tested your capabilities. By now, you're entirely confident that with the right motivation, you can achieve great things and break through barriers that affect everyone.

You possess the potential within you; you just need the right motivation to act against all odds. You've envisioned yourself living this way and know how capable you are. Despite the multitude of options out there, you've given your all to excel on this chosen path.

Frequently ask yourself, is this the life you truly need, or is it a mere fantasy? Do you understand your actions at this level of living? Can you make things happen on this platform, where your mental faculties align with your aspirations? Given the opportunity, would you do anything to become what you desire? Ultimately, you may have no other choice but to immerse yourself in this realm of intelligence.

You completely embrace your idea without needing to replace it with anything else. Even though sometimes it can be painful and uncertain to venture into the unknown and dedicate your life to something uncertain, you remain steadfast in your commitment. Now, the question arises: How far are you willing to go to turn that dream into reality? Achieving your dreams demands your unwavering dedication and comprehension.

Even when obstacles seem insurmountable, you don't shy away from making sacrifices to bring your dreams to fruition. Sometimes, it's the sacrifices we make that pave the way for our desires to become reality. While you may have a sense of what you need to sacrifice, what exactly must you relinquish to shape your love and life as you envision them? What can you let go of, knowing that, regardless of the challenges you face, shedding certain burdens is essential to your growth? Could it be that our very existence is built upon sacrifices, with much being relinquished at birth, making it impossible to attain our goals effortlessly? We must give so much of ourselves, even when it feels like we're pushing ourselves to the limit.

Opportunities to become whatever we wish are rare; instead, we are granted the chance to become what we truly need to be. Despite its difficulties, once you open your heart to a goal, that goal becomes an intrinsic part of you. There's no competition with others; it's your deepest desire you're eager to manifest. As you strive to become the star you're meant to be, the journey may feel somber when mixed with the complexities of the world, but take that singular purpose and shape it into your life.

You will come to know your true self and experience the genuine love that surrounds you. In the vastness of the world, you are presented with a unique opportunity to open the doors to your aspirations. This chance, though rare, transforms into reality. While it may seem like we've already dedicated ourselves to our desires, the inner strength to attain what we truly need may be lacking.

With a deep love for your authentic self and no need for substitutes, you'll sense an untapped potential within, bringing your lifelong goals closer to reality. Even during moments when it appears we're losing touch with our humanity, the genuine desire to become a valuable individual remains.

By putting in effort and patiently awaiting the fruition of your aspirations, you'll witness your true essence materialize. Sometimes, external pressures may be overwhelming, leaving no room for hesitation. In such instances, you must forge ahead on this path, as it's the sole route leading to the fulfillment of your ambitions.

Reflecting upon your journey, it's evident that, without unwavering dedication, you could have easily become lost forever. Yet, by wholeheartedly committing to your growth, you rediscovered yourself and gathered the pieces of your identity. In doing so, you've unveiled aspects of your character previously obscured by life's challenges.

Talent, a precious asset, possesses the power to mend the deepest wounds within a person. Recognizing this gift early on can become a boon to your overall well-being. Embracing the inherent beauty within yourself, you transcend the allure of external accomplishments, ultimately finding contentment unparalleled by any external achievement.

Do we ever find it in ourselves to be just a tad more patient, to allow things to unfold without rushing, because time doesn't always mean falling behind? Occasionally, there's a necessity for personal growth, and when given the space to nurture it, remarkable development takes place, leading to a richer life. It doesn't matter which path you follow; every idea deserves a chance to materialize. Yet, it can be disheartening when you realize you've failed to transform it into success. Regret may consume you, thinking about the potential you could have realized if you had ventured down a different path. It dawns on you that numerous opportunities could have made your life better, had you committed to the right cause. To attain happiness and self-improvement, there's one imperative: strive to be a star.

Discovering your independence and learning to rely on yourself is essential. Accept this truth as soon as possible and make it your guiding principle; otherwise, you may suffer when reality doesn't align with your expectations. Keeping your focus unwaveringly on your goals is vital. With both eyes fixed on your path of creation, without distractions, you can accomplish what's expected of you. Perhaps you've refrained from giving in too easily, seeking to explore different avenues. Now, you constantly question how to liberate your mind from what you've known in order to fulfill your true potential.

Now that you've chosen a new path in life, it's important to acknowledge that your past might try to hold you back from progressing. How long will you let something hinder your progress when you know it's not who you truly are? This can be disheartening and detrimental to your well-being, dragging you down. While it's essential to dedicate yourself to what you love, it's equally important to ensure your journey leads to success and the realization of your dreams.

Sometimes, it may seem like there's a huge obstacle in your way, but don't add unnecessary weight to it; let it stand alone. Learn to cope with the challenges you encounter, as they can wear you out until you're unsure of your next steps. You had the potential to become anything you desired, but external factors have made you realize that you're not only struggling to be yourself but also facing additional difficulties.

Can you focus solely on the path ahead, even if it comes with many challenges? Look away from distractions and concentrate on what can save you from the obstacles in your journey – this could be your salvation, the one thing that can protect you from all that life throws at you.

Many things we do are driven by love, which is the ultimate reward. So, never let your heart be without genuine love. You might not have someone to care for at the moment, but don't allow the importance of what we truly need, which is everything worth living for, to steal your tender heart from that special person who will eventually come into your life. You will encounter someone worthy of your affection, and you will be asked to give something that may be challenging to attain if you haven't practiced caring in your heart regularly. Commitment is a crucial part of our ultimate desire, and you may have failed to find it when it was needed the most, but you will discover a unique soul who complements everything you aspire to be.

We don't simply follow a path; we strive for our ultimate goal, a desire that you will fulfill even though it may not always be easy. You may have faced numerous challenges, and it might have demanded more from you than you initially thought, but in the end, you achieved what your heart desired. Think about how crucial all of this has been in your life, as it encompasses everything worth living for. You might have felt stuck at times, for reasons that didn't make sense, but once you embrace what you truly desire, you'll see that all the unnecessary aspects of your life will fade away.

Why must we subject ourselves to something that never brings us happiness? Often, we find ourselves grappling with challenges that may exist only in our thoughts, caused by different mindsets, old notions, or dominant mentalities that influence our thinking. Yet, the solution lies within reach. All we need to do is let go of our past selves, shed the weight of old age, and journey towards a new understanding of how to manifest our desires. By diligently working to transform undesirable aspects of ourselves and embracing change, we create space for positive outcomes.

The culmination of our efforts can ultimately vindicate the pain, frustration, and confusion endured along the way, as we inch closer to our goals. This process allows us to lead a life we truly cherish, breathing life into our existence. We begin to experience the essence of our humanity, an irreplaceable feeling no one can strip from our hearts. Yet, we may wonder, can pursuing a goal or fulfilling a need truly be detrimental, capable of forever tainting our lives? As we reflect on our transformation, it may seem as though the pain will never recede, but perhaps it can dissipate. Often, we carry burdens too heavy in our hearts, allowing them to overshadow the essence of who we once were.

When you have a goal to achieve, it's important to ensure that it doesn't rely too heavily on others. Instead, choose something you can accomplish independently, drawing upon your own abilities and knowledge. Failing to become what you aspire to be can have profound consequences, potentially leading to a loss of your essential humanity. To avoid this, you should place your utmost trust in yourself, as doing so opens the doors to a fulfilling life.

Many aspects of your journey cannot be achieved solely through the capabilities of others. Therefore, it's essential to find inner peace in the knowledge that you have the capacity to achieve these goals on your own, often reaching heights beyond the comprehension of many.

The world won't hand you success; you must create it for yourself. No one will force you into a role you're not capable of fulfilling. When you venture forth, push yourself to the highest level, fully aware that you're dedicating your life to something you're willing to make sacrifices for. The resources you need are within you, and with determination in your heart, you can accomplish almost anything. You can initiate and complete projects, infusing them with meaning without external interference.

Being like stars in the sky, we inherently know how to bring out our best. We feel it within us and choose to pursue everything necessary to enrich our lives. Failing to understand how to become self-sufficient is difficult to justify. So, practice this understanding, have unwavering faith in yourself, forge a path even in the absence of one, and, in the end, reward yourself by acknowledging that it was your capabilities and knowledge that drove your success.

Chapter Eight

Fearless

What could be more challenging than stepping into the world to seize the opportunities life offers, thanks to our incredible ability to comprehend the world around us? One of the primary obstacles we often encounter on our journey to personal growth is the limitations we impose upon ourselves due to our own thoughts. These self-imposed constraints can prevent us from realizing our full potential. While our potential is vast, our perceptions can greatly influence our progress, making it difficult to break free from self-imposed restrictions.

Many individuals experience this sensation, wherein they grapple with the quest to align their inner selves with their external personas over an extended period. This persistent question may revolve around fears of missing out on life's opportunities due to apprehensions.

Perhaps you worry that pursuing your passions will compel you to engage socially, a prospect that may fill you with anxiety about interacting with others, sharing your thoughts, and expressing your opinions. It's possible that you find it challenging to embrace the world as it is. You may feel as though you're constantly on guard against potential threats, holding you back from achieving your goals. To achieve your objectives, it's crucial to recognize that we all belong to a free society where individuals have the right to express themselves in any manner they choose.

In a world where it's important to be yourself and share your thoughts, when you venture out, you should be ready to reveal who you are. When you step out into the world, you're representing your unique perspective, a part of what you hold dear, or perhaps something many are uncertain about – their beliefs in society. People often fear the potential impact of their own creations, and this fear weakens many. They don't become as strong as they could be in embodying what they're made of. They lack the courage to stand up and discuss what they are most passionate about.

How can you overcome this fear that holds us back from so many things? How do you reach a point where you understand that by standing up, you're not only endorsing a particular idea but also representing the beliefs of many others who share your viewpoint? It's important to acknowledge that your ideas may clash with others, and this might make you question your own convictions. In such situations, it's crucial to be considerate of others and their perspectives on life. Not everyone subscribes to the same beliefs, so when you express your opinions, do so in a way that respects other people's viewpoints. Learning to adapt to this is essential.

What are we truly afraid of that prevents us from pursuing our dreams with ease? There may come a time when you feel diminished by circumstances, so much so that you wish to retreat from everything. Occasionally, you may find yourself uncertain about the world, especially since people perceive it differently. It's possible to perceive the world as a daunting place when you go out to confront reality. It can feel like something is poised to overwhelm you, potentially depriving you of the opportunity to showcase your talents for an extended period.

When you keep your ideas confined within your mind, unsure if they are right or wrong, it's essential to consider taking action. Starting your own path is a positive step if you believe in your thoughts. However, you can't stay hidden forever; eventually, you must share your ideas with others for their judgment. In life, we often face resistance, like swimming against a strong current, but it's crucial to persevere and strive for success.

There comes a moment when you need to leave behind self-imposed limitations and embrace change, becoming the person you are meant to be. Deep inside, you might hold a dream that requires pursuit. Ignoring that part of your life due to fear would let fear control you indefinitely. You may have wished for more but hesitated because of uncertainty about what lies ahead, feeling constrained as if something might stifle or erase you.

Now, you live with doubts, fearing potential failure and the waste of your life's potential. You wonder if pursuing your dreams will lead to success or not. This uncertainty might deter you, keeping you from realizing your full potential. Even if the journey doesn't offer everything you desire, it's often better to persevere rather than venture into the unknown. Change can be intimidating, and its significance should not be underestimated, as it hinges on acting on your thoughts and aspirations.

Sometimes, finding the courage to pursue everything you love in the life you're living can be a bit challenging. You may hesitate at times, but the key is to go after your passions with confidence, drawing upon all the knowledge and experiences you've gathered. Occasionally, when you're not entirely knowledgeable or well-versed in a subject, it can lead to a lack of self-assurance. You may feel uncertain because you haven't fully mastered a topic. When someone questions your viewpoint, it can feel intimidating, as though they are prying into your knowledge, which can make you uneasy about what you don't know.

Much of what we don't comprehend about life, as well as our gaps in knowledge, can be frustrating and overwhelming. This is particularly true when you must share your understanding with others. You might wonder why you lack confidence in presenting your thoughts to the world. Perhaps you are uncertain whether your knowledge is sufficient or if you excel in your endeavors, and this uncertainty can be difficult to justify. When you're not consistently content with what you're doing, it can negatively impact your life, causing you to withdraw from participation.

It's important to stay receptive to different ideas that people have, even though your own ideas matter. You just need to put in extra effort to shine. We all possess unique talents that can be like a hidden treasure within us. Allowing these talents to emerge may not be easy, especially if you're unsure about how to stand out compared to others. Take a moment to reflect: Are you not just like everyone else? What steps can you take to enhance your life and boost your competence?

You can't be perfect for every person due to their unique beliefs and lifestyles, but you can strive to have a deep understanding of various aspects of life.

It's important to be mindful of the world around you and surprise people by providing what they desire, even if they didn't anticipate it. Achieving greatness is within your reach. We're all human, and sometimes we hold limiting views of life, but we also know we can do better. When you possess the determination to improve, remarkable things can happen, driven by your desires.

To thrive in a complex world, it's crucial to adapt early rather than waiting until it's too late. You might end up becoming well-known for something unexpected. Life rarely unfolds as anticipated, and discovering your true self can be challenging. You might question your abilities and compare yourself unfavorably to others, but remember, you have a unique purpose that involves shining brightly.

Your primary goal should be to give your all, consistently pushing your limits. This effort will enable you to break through barriers and achieve levels no one thought possible. However, success won't occur by accident; it must be something you genuinely desire. Demonstrating unwavering dedication to your passions is essential. If something means so much to you, don't tire of pursuing it. Ultimately, your commitment to your passions will define you and your legacy.

Hard work and dedication can be powerful tools that help you break free and achieve your goals in all aspects of life. If you aspire to become something more, don't pursue your endeavors solely for personal pleasure. At some point in your journey, allocate considerable attention to your pursuits, treating them as if your well-being hinges on them. Maintain this enthusiasm consistently; don't let your determination wane over a short period. Only find satisfaction when you've reached your destination and exceeded your expectations. Regardless of your chosen path, your unwavering commitment will always be evident in your passion.

Every effort you invest will yield meaningful results, especially in creative pursuits. Keep your focus on these endeavors. Sometimes, we hold onto things out of belief but fail to take purposeful action. Avoid getting stuck in situations where success remains elusive. The best phases of our lives should allow us to fully embrace and be content with our true selves. Recognize and appreciate the inherent qualities that define you; these are aspects you cannot change.

Enthusiasm is an indispensable quality within a person that should guide your journey. Perform your work and fulfill your life's roles because they bring out your best self. Don't embark on endeavors out of desperation for financial gain, especially if it holds no real meaning for you. Authentic commitment should be at the core of everything you undertake, to the extent that it becomes an integral part of your identity. Pursue your passions wholeheartedly and discover the incredible potential that emerges when fueled by the spirit of understanding and dedication.

When we infuse our actions with genuine love at their core, these efforts won't go unnoticed. This is where people converge, and a profound comprehension unfolds. It all begins with taking a firm stance. Do not forsake your devotion while expecting to evolve into a significant individual. Leaving behind your potential is a missed opportunity. Communicate in a universally comprehensible language, allowing others to recognize their own aspirations within your endeavors.

Neglecting love obscures our path and hinders humanity from attaining true insight. Any portion you omit may lead to future remorse. Our existence finds purpose in that pivotal juncture, where reciprocity thrives—what you offer, you receive. This is how you garner admiration, channeling authentic love into your innermost desires, with returns magnified within your work.

True dedication completes our endeavors, providing meaning in all our pursuits. Refrain from doubting such commitment in your undertakings, for living without understanding its significance may render life futile. You might dwell in obscurity, lost within the core of reality, seeking self-discovery but finding only uncertainty. Occasionally, dedicate your time to a cherished passion, driven by the core of your heart. This resonates globally, shaping the perception of who you are. The true essence remains elusive until you wholeheartedly commit.

You might be surprised to discover that some of the most challenging situations can lose their power when we approach them with genuine love and dedication. This is the key element you should invest your life in. When you engage in an activity, it's essential to recognize the deep devotion you feel for it, driving you to act with unwavering commitment. True purpose often emerges when you wholeheartedly devote yourself to your work, allowing your inner love to propel you toward success.

Our innermost desires serve as the conduit through which our aspirations flow. By embracing what we don't yet understand and acknowledging how it affects our progress, we can overcome our fears. It's this lack of understanding that often hinders us from effortlessly pursuing our chosen paths.

Is there something profound about life that you're hesitant to share with others? Knowledge serves as our solid foundation for navigating the world around us. When we adopt this perspective, life becomes the bridge connecting us to everyone and everything in our environment. In truth, our daily experiences are largely shaped by our interests and focus.

What you're searching for makes you question everything you already know. The feedback we receive has shaped the impression we've left on people. Without us and our way of life, others might not care about us or be curious about our actions. As we strive for self-improvement, it's crucial not to dwell on our past failures. Instead, seek connections between your feelings about the world and your aspirations.

Don't leave any part of yourself behind; ensure that all aspects of your being progress together. To attain your desires, put in diligent and sustained effort to navigate challenges that may seem daunting. Although we often arrive at our destinations through different paths, it's essential to periodically evaluate your own integrity and self-identity along the way. This introspection is the culmination of your experiences and love.

These experiences will shape your ambitions in ways you might not have imagined when you initially felt lost and unsure about achieving your goals. Over time, clarity emerges as you learn how to focus your thoughts and feelings with devotion.

Search for your inner self, the repository of wisdom and knowledge. Intelligence enhances our beauty and brings out our best as human beings. You aren't truly lost; you're still on your journey. The more you push towards your goals, the deeper your understanding becomes, allowing you to embrace your authentic self. Perhaps you were once lost, but now you've found yourself through your innermost desires. The question you must answer is, 'How do you propel your ambitions to reach your destination?'

Whether you realize it or not, the journey to becoming a complete human being unfolds in front of you once you reach your destination, no matter which path you take. This journey encompasses everything necessary for life, and it's not just about excelling in one aspect but fulfilling all your needs. Yes, it might seem challenging, but it's an honest challenge that pushes you to attain the reality you desire. Ultimately, your true essence cannot be taken away from you; it's a testament to your willpower and capabilities.

You have the opportunity to offer the best version of yourself right now and seize the present moment, becoming a strong and confident individual. It might appear that dedicating yourself entirely to one aspect of life is your only choice, but that's because you've invested your entire being in it, and there's no one else to blame. If it's your passion, it should be your primary focus. You don't have to wait until you've exhausted all other options to realize that discipline can help you achieve it. Consider everything you know as a tool to reach your goals, and perhaps it's time to understand that your survival hinges on utilizing every opportunity presented to you.

View each day as a chance for personal growth along the path that exists in your mind. Life can be seen from this perspective, leading to personal salvation and transformation into what you genuinely aspire to become. Even when facing adversity, there's always a breakthrough waiting to happen, and that's how you capitalize on it. Sometimes, the smallest elements shape our lives. This transformation is likely to occur before we reach the point where our true essence becomes something significant and meaningful enough for others to witness.

If you don't gather those small pieces and use them to create something amazing, no one will be able to understand your vision. Dreams are quite challenging to turn into reality. They often stay in our minds for a long time without becoming real. Many of our hopes and visions remain just thoughts because they lack the power to become true. Sometimes, you might need a push to do what's necessary, but true discipline on your journey will help you make your dreams come to life. Remember, everyone starts somewhere, and you know where you are right now. Learn to succeed in different areas and thrive. Your life is like a foundation; collect your strengths and put them to good use. You might not realize how capable you are or how far you can go, so push through any obstacles.

Becoming a star is a unique chance to make a difference in life. Don't doubt your feelings about what you want to become. Deep down, you know how to be everything you love about this world. You don't need someone to teach you; the determination you have inside is crucial for your journey. It includes your strength, courage, commitment, and the perseverance you need to reach your goals.

You'll know you're on the right path when you have a deep love driving you. When you love something deeply and give it your all to turn it into reality, that's when you've truly arrived. You desired something so strongly that you didn't even need a teacher; the path became clearer, showing you how to reach your destination. You battled against your old self until you became the person you wanted to be. Despite the obstacles that often hold us back, you've overcome them and reached the other side.

While we appreciate having control over our lives, we also believe in fate, the idea that some things are destined to happen just the way they do. This belief suggests that even though we might have envisioned a different path, the way things unfold often leads to positive outcomes that shape our character. It's a way of understanding and accepting the losses we encounter in life. Although you may have wished for happiness in every aspect of your existence, sometimes reality doesn't align with our desires, and it can leave you feeling behind, yearning for a more conventional progression.

This feeling of falling behind can serve as a catalyst for personal transformation, propelling you towards your ultimate goals and a happiness that surpasses anything you've known. Our journey towards happiness is closely tied to the choices we make and the paths we take. Your enthusiasm for life, your affection for someone special, and your commitment to keeping that person in your life all contribute to your sense of self. Unlike times when you may have held back or hesitated, this time, you've given yourself completely to the moment. You cherish every aspect of your current self, determined not to lose your identity to something else. This moment marks a crucial point in your journey, where your deepest desires become reality, and you've welcomed a wealth of emotions into your heart.

Initially, we are born with limited knowledge about ourselves, but our hearts are filled with boundless love for who we are. This self-acceptance is a cornerstone of human happiness. Even as we strive towards our dreams, we sometimes overlook essential aspects of ourselves, leaving us feeling empty. It's crucial to gather the fragments of our lives, tap into our inner strength, and cultivate a profound capacity for love. This love enables us to see the world through a different lens, while hatred only turns us away. Instead, confront your fears and embrace your true self, for completeness requires embracing all that you are.

When you venture out into the world, you seek to rediscover the missing fragments of your heart and soul. It doesn't matter how badly you've been hurt or knocked down. Even when life has dealt its harshest blows, it's by committing to our aspirations that we genuinely uncover our true selves. What causes us to lose touch with our inner essence? Is it because we mistakenly believe we're all alike? The reality is, we're all unique, and each circumstance affects us differently. The moment you start perceiving yourself differently, you're on the path to healing and self-discovery.

Everything occurring around us contributes to shaping a fundamental part of who we are deep inside, but we each take a distinct form. Our past experiences, our present circumstances, and our aspirations for the future sculpt and define our life journeys. Otherwise, we'd all extract the same essence from life, regardless of our perspectives or vantage points. Yet, we discover that we're not identical, and we're often perplexed about how we've reached our current positions. Although we begin with similar resources in life, their impact varies due to our individuality, our locations, and the choices we make.

You're aware that you deserve more, much more. However, your current way of life isn't providing the satisfaction you seek. So, take a moment to reflect: What might you be doing incorrectly? Where could you be missing the mark on the path to genuine happiness in life? Don't turn your gaze away from yourself; your true self resides within. Despite our tendency to search for meaning in all the wrong places, reach deep within, for your inner essence is within arm's reach.

Our progress and perspective depend on many factors. At times, we may have been unaware of what we should focus on. It's only when certain events or experiences occur that we begin to grasp our true selves. There might be moments when we blame ourselves for not realizing certain things earlier. However, we come to understand that it's because we weren't fully prepared for the challenges life threw our way. When we become disciplined and ready, we start seeing each day as an opportunity.

From that point onward, we appreciate every moment as a gift. We develop a mindset that views each day as a chance for personal growth. When a day becomes a source of pride and an opportunity to seize, we recognize our blessings. We comprehend that as long as we have our life and knowledge, no situation is truly insurmountable. Once we've studied diligently, our mind becomes our primary tool for clarity and making the most of every situation.

Even in your youth, when the world can be confusing, there's no need to blame yourself for what you may have lost. Instead, consider making peace with the circumstances that have brought you to this point in your journey. Time has undoubtedly played a role in shaping you and influencing your choices. Think about all the potential paths your life could have taken, and realize that you've arrived at this moment seeking self-understanding and closure.

To achieve success, it's essential to accept your present circumstances and acknowledge how they connect your past and future. Amid the wonder of life and the pursuit of knowledge, you continue searching for your true self. Only through discipline can you piece together the fragments of your identity and mend the damage that time may have caused. Practicing discipline in applying the knowledge you've gained is crucial to finding your purpose.

We have the potential to achieve so much through the knowledge we've acquired on our individual journeys. However, at times, we may lose our way, diverting our attention to things unworthy of our focus. Placing our trust in our own abilities is a valuable asset, but it demands our utmost respect in everything we undertake. Our lives are fundamentally our own responsibility, and much is at stake.

Part of this wisdom may elude us initially, as it isn't typically gained on the first day of our journey. We may tread a long path without grasping the secrets of success. Along this route, we learn that assuming responsibility for our well-being is just the beginning. Success is not a product of chance; it emerges when we remain unwaveringly committed and well-informed in our pursuits, knowing how to turn our efforts into tangible results.

Yet, this journey forces us to question our knowledge and understanding. But, we mustn't abandon the life we've diligently built. Our way of life is not inherently wrong; it simply requires us to cling steadfastly to the pillars of success when we're charting our own course. Every day presents a wealth of opportunities and blessings, as well as potential pitfalls and challenges. It's up to us to decide which path we wish to tread.

Within our minds, we hold the power to navigate these diverse pathways and bear the consequences of our choices. We can choose to immerse ourselves in a world brimming with opportunities and blessings or journey down a perilous road laden with traps and hardships. The choice is entirely ours to make. So, how would you like to shape your existence? Do you aspire to live a life enriched with blessings and opportunities, or are you veering down the treacherous path of curses and traps, ultimately leading to failure?

Enhance the depth of meaning by grasping the intended way of things, and you'll discover that success has always been within your reach, requiring nothing more than discipline. It might have taken considerable effort to grasp this truth, but you shouldn't let yourself hinder your own progress. Overcome the internal obstacles, and you'll find that external challenges fade away. The world can be tough, and it demands knowledge and understanding, but with discipline as your guide, you'll never be insignificant if you excel in your role.

However, achieving ultimate success is not guaranteed; making every day count is a key to success. You'll truly comprehend this through the actions you consistently apply to your daily work. It's possible to miss the meaning, but you must recognize that your chances of triumph are substantial and ever-present, although they may not be apparent unless you adopt a prosperity-driven mindset.

Don't be fearful of the world, for failure is not predetermined. Hard work will propel you toward that point in life where you'll fully grasp your purpose. We are each endowed with unique qualities, akin to stars, to experience our distinct realities. When you open your eyes and explore the world, you'll discover the opportunities it offers. You've been granted the chance to become anything you desire, but the vastness of possibilities may prompt you to question your worthiness.

You cannot inherently fail; everything depends on your efforts, and achieving success rests in your hands. Why embark on a certain path only to squander it? Don't cling to outdated notions after your past has passed; we aren't born with all the knowledge we need, and we all make a few mistakes along the way, but many of them can be rectified. With perseverance, you can attain what you desire in the end. It may seem like destiny, as if it was meant to be, and that's how you can justify finding meaning in the end.

Chapter Nine

Change the World

Each one of us has a specific role in life, regardless of who we are or what we do. We have the potential to make a positive impact on our community or change someone's life, particularly those who are in dire need of our presence. There may be times when you feel disconnected from your purpose, and this can lead to a sense of disintegration within yourself.

This occurs when you struggle with self-acceptance and lack the motivation to contribute your true self to the world around you. It's ironic that by withdrawing from active participation and not giving your best to the world, you end up losing your own identity.

We have a lot to care for, and sometimes it's through selflessness and dedicating ourselves to everything around us that we discover our true calling. Although resisting our true selves may feel comforting, especially to those who rely on us, caring opens the door for countless opportunities to flourish within us. This is a valuable lesson that doesn't come without effort.

Caring teaches us about the intricacies of life and how to take responsibility, not only for those who require our assistance but also for our own well-being. Growing is a daily responsibility, and it's crucial to comprehend how to shape our lives as we desire, lest we lose sight of what truly matters.

The responsibilities we neglect can transform into vulnerabilities, weakening us from within and diminishing our sense of self-worth, ultimately rendering our lives devoid of meaning.

We all have hearts, and sometimes these hearts can cause harm to those we come close to. Even the people we love the most can end up getting hurt by our actions. Living without understanding can become a habit, but it's the people we hurt who feel the pain of our actions. You might think that hurting others will help you achieve your goals, but in reality, it often doesn't go as planned. Eventually, you might find yourself stuck, unable to get what you want, and you might blame the world for not caring about your desires.

So, what have you neglected that has made things seem so impossible? We all have our own reasons and motivations for our actions, but who are we hurting in the process? Who needs us the most? It's not just about who needs us; the world demands a lot from us as well. Sometimes, it's important to reflect on what matters most to us: love, care, and who depends on us for support. While we may want to be loved by everyone, there are those who need us the most, and by reaching out to them, we can find fulfillment in our lives.

Happiness comes from embracing the best parts of ourselves, those qualities we are meant to cherish throughout our lives. Sometimes, the world can be confusing, and we allow it to influence our thoughts and actions, causing us to lose sight of what truly matters. We expose ourselves to too much, which can lead to self-absorption as we chase our ambitions. We open ourselves to distractions that confuse our sense of reality. Instead, it's essential to focus on what brings us back to our true selves.

While we have the capacity to love and share a piece of ourselves with those who rely on us, it's important to recognize that negative energies can undermine the relationships we cherish. Understanding the potential pitfalls can be challenging, as the path ahead may not be familiar. Sometimes, we resist aspects of ourselves that could hinder us from discovering true love. Ultimately, it's us who will bear the discomfort and unhappiness when we can't find someone to commit to.

In truth, deep within, we possess self-awareness about our identity and the pain stemming from unmet desires. Our hearts may struggle to cope with challenging circumstances. Determining what's truly essential can be uncertain—

whether we should downplay our goals or persevere despite the burdens they impose. Must we desire so much at the expense of love, especially when its absence makes us feel abandoned by the world? Yet, failing at everything can intensify our longing for improvement, where love could have been a preferable choice.

Perhaps we neglect those who love and depend on us, even more dishearteningly, we do this to ourselves after others have placed immense trust in us. Despite our self-assurances, we may prioritize our objectives and responsibilities, intending to demonstrate our love and concern once these are addressed. Our desires often overshadow the urgent needs of the world, which require our attention now, not in the future. This moment, while we are young and capable, is when we can truly make a difference.

When you are confident that life is what you know and what you pursue, when deep within you, you possess the power to effect change. We are granted a sufficient amount of strength from one point to another to rectify situations, to manage all that is required. Beyond that, if we neglect something that demands our attention, everything starts to crumble. Among those who bear the burden of your actions are the ones you should hold dear and cherish.

There may be uncertainties at times, but when you finally understand, when love begins to resonate in your heart, demonstrate your affection and concern. Because opportunities don't last forever, and the reasons for being present may not always be clear. However, you don't have to wait until your world falls apart and the challenges become insurmountable.

Instead, you can rationalize the purpose of living the life you lead. Sometimes, we may be justified, as people can wrong us to a point where forgiveness is not easy. Nevertheless, when God has bestowed a gift upon you, utilize it to give life, harness it, and touch the lives of those who surround you. At times, our minds can encompass all of humanity, and instead of tormenting others with your knowledge, show them kindness.

Many negative influences impact us due to what we witness, and this pain may penetrate deep into our hearts, lingering from past experiences. Yet, why choose to inflict harm? Why cause such pain to others, who may even be innocent in the situation? Instead, extend mercy to them. You could have been the person who loves or cares for them.

Yes, at times, it can be challenging to accept certain situations when you reflect on what you might have lost and what you could have had. It can be confusing, and you may feel a deep sadness for enduring such hardship. This pain can become overwhelming and transform us into someone we are not. However, it's important to realize that harming yourself will only result in more suffering, hindering your ability to embody the goodness you aspire to. Life often requires us to learn the art of forgiveness and move forward by leaving the past behind.

If you observe your surroundings closely, you will recognize that there is a great need for love and compassion, especially if you genuinely consider yourself a person with a loving heart. Therefore, do not abandon those close to you, even when doubts arise. As you approach the end of your journey, you will comprehend the importance of caring for others. Many are yearning for your attention and support in their lives.

Do not turn your back on genuine love and focus solely on those who harbor animosity towards you. While we aspire to love, we must acknowledge that nothing in life comes without its challenges. Even when our intentions are pure, we may encounter obstacles that challenge our beliefs and knowledge. The world outside is not always accommodating to everyone, which can be a source of frustration for many.

Ultimately, everything unfolds as it should. The only misconception is the belief that life should always be easy. When faced with difficulty, we tend to accept defeat or contemplate destructive actions. However, it's essential to understand that what you desire may clash with the reality of the world. Instead of nurturing hatred and destructive thoughts, remember that your desires will inevitably collide with the complexities of existence.

You can discover life's lessons in different ways, either through challenging experiences or smoother paths, especially when you grow older and life seems less vibrant. It's a sobering realization that life can be complex, with numerous mysteries to unravel. You might ponder whether you truly grasp the significance of your actions. When did the world become so bewildering? If you were faced with overwhelming difficulties, would you know how to stay true to your ideals? Would you persevere in holding onto your values amidst adversity? The way things unfold may hinge on your ability to adapt and the choices you make from the myriad of possibilities.

We, as humans, often find ourselves ill-equipped to deal with such unforeseen setbacks. The struggle to attain our deepest desires is not our natural state. We are ordinary individuals who yearn to pursue our most cherished aspirations without sacrificing our essence. We hold onto that inner child, the dreamer who once envisioned this world full of possibilities. Yet, as life narrows down to pursuing that singular dream, you realize you will confront every challenge the world throws at you to make that dream a reality.

As you approach the culmination of your journey, can you maintain a clear distinction between your aspirations and your capacity to love, all while preserving your inner tranquility and authenticity? Perhaps what people truly need is a guide who has weathered countless storms and navigated treacherous terrain. This guide could be anyone—a family member, a fellow citizen, or perhaps you, with your unique story. However, before reaching that role, you must overcome numerous obstacles for which you were unprepared. Nevertheless, there's no need to harbor resentment toward the world. Instead, demonstrate your profound care, understanding who you are and the sacrifices you've made. Although it may have been a challenging journey, your story can provide others with cause for celebration.

To forgive the world means understanding your own identity. It's about convincing yourself and taking responsibility for the role you play in people's lives. If you're a leader, you must lead and realize that who you are might not align with everyone else's reality. You perceive the world differently, as if its inner workings have become more transparent to you. Therefore, you should embrace the challenges and accept things as they are, recognizing that they are meant for your growth. Feel the sorrow of those who look up to you, and live your life with gratitude and honor. Don't give up or shy away from your responsibilities. Aim to think like the person you aspire to become.

Living with this mindset, you should be prepared for the hardships that may come your way. If you ever turn a blind eye, it could lead to suffering for many. It's important to bear their pain and shoulder their burdens because you understand that going through tough times can tear their souls apart, causing immense suffering. These challenges are meant to make us stronger individuals, encouraging us to pursue our goals despite the formidable obstacles we face, even though victory won't come overnight.

Nevertheless, you should persist in your efforts, working diligently to confront the daily challenges of life. Be the one who accepts the reality of the world as it is, and others will learn from your example. There's no better time than the present to step onto the platform of your dreams. By leading and caring for others, we guide ourselves towards the destination we've always longed for.

Sometimes, it doesn't matter how you ended up in a difficult place where everything feels like a struggle. Regardless of how sad it may make you feel, forgiveness might be necessary. Life can be tough to bear at times, and there's a limit to how much we can endure. We're not always prepared for what lies ahead. However, facing these challenges teaches us resilience, allowing us to endure the pain, frustration, and confusion that fill our lives.

What defines us as individuals is our ability to turn away from negativity and embrace love. Love is the core of your identity, so make sure to cultivate it within your heart abundantly. Transform yourself into a reservoir of greatness by practicing care and understanding. Remember that nothing will ever be sufficient, and you'll always encounter challenges. In such times, give yourself completely, knowing that you should return to the inner sanctuary where you've saved yourself. This place can help you perceive the world from a new perspective.

It's essential to recognize that hatred often casts a shadow over our lives. Yet, deep down, we understand that we aren't the negative images people may try to shape us into. We are humble individuals with kind hearts. Therefore, let your actions be influenced by this truth. Many of life's trials attempt to mold us into something we're not. This prompts us to reflect on our choices and the pressures they impose. Are we losing touch with our true selves?

Are we being pushed beyond our limits, forced to forsake the love that forgives the world for its flaws? Live with the knowledge that the world has always been as it is, and you didn't create its imperfections. There are aspects of life beyond our control, and we must accept them. You tried to build your world on an existing foundation, and when you couldn't find your place, it felt overwhelming.

Where can you find the strength to face everything, accept the daily challenges, and continue living without letting hatred take hold? You may feel tainted by your actions and disconnected from humanity, lingering in darkness as long as you live, overshadowed by difficulties. If the world hasn't met your expectations, now is the time to decide how to move forward. Many things may hold you back, but your response can shape your journey.

Strive to become what you've always dreamed of, even if obstacles and challenges have transformed your aspirations into something complex. What actions would you take if no other option remained available to you? Your response to this question, your deepest desires, may require unwavering belief and unshakable faith in achieving the seemingly impossible. Endeavor to break free from the constraints of adversity, and, if necessary, employ sheer determination to bring your aspirations to fruition. Refuse to yield to external pressures that would reshape you into something you are not.

We are human beings destined for greatness, yet there are moments when everything appears at risk unless we muster the courage to confront the most daunting circumstances and infuse our lives with extraordinary accomplishments. The origins of our journey may be insignificant, but the destination we set our sights on is what truly counts. Even when life has been plagued by misfortune and letdowns, it becomes essential to acknowledge the person you have evolved into. Forge your path, no matter the sacrifices, knowing that every endeavor fueled by love in your heart will yield profound transformations and surpass your wildest expectations.

The profound lesson to remember is that certain challenges may be directed squarely at you, aiming for the core of your being. In such moments, reflect on whether you have cultivated the resilience necessary to endure the trials of existence. When you prepare for life's myriad challenges, do so with the understanding that your efforts are meant to safeguard you against the full spectrum of adversities that loom. Numerous forces may conspire to unsettle you and provoke the darkest aspects of your character, and it can be a daunting prospect to accept that you are not alone in this struggle. Yet, many individuals merely accept their circumstances and learn to coexist with them.

If you want to feel better, just take a moment to look outside and see what's around you. If you notice things aren't great, that's okay. The key to achieving great things is being prepared for the challenges that lie ahead on your journey. Don't fool yourself into thinking things will magically get better. Sometimes, they won't change at all, and you'll have to face the harsh reality.

If you're not ready for what's out there, your whole life could be in jeopardy. So, don't hesitate. Embrace the truth and be willing to change yourself with the knowledge you have.

No matter how long you've neglected your responsibilities, the important thing is that you've finally realized the need for change. Every day brings new opportunities to improve our lives, regardless of our past negligence. What matters now is that you're taking steps to make things right. You may have overlooked many aspects of yourself, but it's not too late to make a change.

Consider it a fresh start, a chance to contribute positively to the world and the lives of those you care about. You still have much to offer, and it's never too late to start making a difference.

We all have a part of ourselves that needs to care deeply about something. This caring feeling brings with it a sense of responsibility. When you have someone in your life who means a lot to you, you'll understand how to excel. When you live knowing that there are people you truly love, you wouldn't want to let them down. It's clear that if there's anyone who looks up to you and sees you as a source of strength, it would deeply hurt you when these innocent faces suffer because of your own mistakes. We're not afraid to face challenges for our own sake. It's when you don't have anyone to care for that you can become indifferent to the many facets of life out there.

Sometimes, you may feel like giving up on yourself. There might be moments when you lack the motivation to expand your horizons and explore new frontiers. However, when there's another soul that relies on you and believes in you, you don't have much of a choice. We all have responsibilities, and these commitments help us realize our own worth. It's not just about giving to those who depend on or love us; it's also about giving to ourselves.

The moment you abandon those you love, you lose hope in everything that truly matters. It might not become apparent immediately, but eventually, you'll experience a great deal of hardship. That's when you stop trying. However, when we have reasons to hold on to life, it gives us a purpose to stay alive, strong, and focused on our goals.

You have a choice to make: you can stay where you are or decide to move forward in your life, becoming someone who lives up to their potential. Refusing to handle your responsibilities means missing out on opportunities for personal growth. Responsibilities are like guiding lights that keep us on track toward our goals. Even if you're not obsessively chasing success, having goals in mind is how we stay motivated and alive, always striving to improve ourselves.

Life can throw obstacles our way, trying to hold us back and weigh us down. To stay alive and thrive, you need a genuine purpose. All it takes is a reason why and for whom you're doing it. It might be challenging, but remind yourself of your reasons, even if you can't change the whole world. For those dear to your heart, the ones you love and care for, nurturing them will help you grow and find your place in this world.

Growth is a responsibility we all embrace. Without things we value, life loses its meaning, and you might feel lost within yourself. Not all battles need to be fought, but if you focus on what truly matters to you, life can become more manageable. Ask yourself: Who do I love and care about the most? Who might need my support to overcome their challenges? Embracing responsibilities helps us navigate tough situations, defining the essence of life itself.

Living with purpose becomes the answer to life's questions, keeping everything that tries to steal our vitality at bay.

No matter what you do or who you aspire to become, do not let hatred take root in your heart, for it can make your path more challenging. Hatred can divert your focus and hinder personal growth. It often leads us away from the richness of life, undermining our purpose as human beings. Regardless of how you've started your journey, consider it a vital part of your identity. Our responsibilities serve as benchmarks of our normalcy.

Set clear goals and commit to them. Even when faced with difficulties, hold onto your objectives. Resist the temptation to let negativity take residence within you. It's easy to lose sight of your true self, but your responsibilities help maintain your sense of humanity. If you have a duty to care for your family, do so with an open heart. If you are entrusted with leadership, guide others to preserve their essence, as this is what defines us as human beings.

Sometimes, we should embrace our circumstances and recognize that the burdens we carry can dignify our lives. Avoid self-hatred; instead, let it teach you to love and care genuinely, rejecting pleasure derived from the suffering of others. Don't revel in the misfortunes of those around you. When you genuinely care, you find a purpose worth living for, steering your entire being in the right direction.

When you do something for someone, they become a part of your life, adding value and strength to everything you do. On the other hand, when someone neglects you, they remove you from their life. So, choose wisely and care for the people close to you. Let them help you through tough times. Offering kindness is not too much of a burden; it's a small responsibility that contributes to the support you receive.

The people in your life provide the strength you need to face your fears.

Don't let anything change who you are on the inside. You could lose a significant part of yourself if you do. Along the way, you might notice that there are forces trying to diminish the kindness in your heart. When we show love to those who truly need it, we are often accepted and receive love in return. It's not fear that brings us what we desire most; it's caring. Just be there when someone needs you, and you'll receive the same in return.

We often complain about not achieving our goals and working tirelessly to make something big happen. However, have you ever considered that your self-centered focus might be the reason you're not winning or achieving your goals? If, for a moment, you can put aside the idea of winning and focus on giving to those in need without worrying about who you're helping, you might find a sense of belonging. Your true self can be embraced when you do so.

We aren't designed to operate solely in our comfort zones. Our true purpose extends beyond harboring hatred or disdain for those who care about us or those we believe should care for us. Numerous questions can be challenging to address, such as what defines our identity or what leads us to a fulfilling life. Is there anyone out there who possesses the keys to what we hold most dear? Perhaps not. Yet, we possess the potential to shape our own destinies, equipped with the answers to the daily inquiries we encounter. Even when faced with rejection by others, it is imperative to remain true to oneself. Our compassionate nature should remain unwavering, as it was at the outset, and our commitment to humanity's welfare must endure.

If your destiny involves love, then love more passionately than you did yesterday, regardless of the obstacles that attempt to hinder your progress. Embrace the trials of existence in order to witness your life's unfolding. Achieving your aspirations may not be a daily occurrence; it often requires patience, and you may linger in anticipation for an extended period. Nevertheless, if it is destined to materialize, it will, regardless of the duration it takes. Always bear in mind that success ultimately outweighs all else, regardless of the time it takes for a particular dream to materialize. What truly matters is recognizing the path to manifesting your desires and the potential for a joyful future.

Cultivate a generous heart capable of accommodating life's vicissitudes, regardless of their potential impact on you. Become a refuge for those who differ from you. We are not inherently equipped for the complexities of life, so forgive yourself for not starting as a master. Some aspects of our identity are inherited, and understanding oneself may not be immediately apparent without introspection. We inherit our essence and embark on a continuous journey of self-discovery, occasionally encountering turbulence that can divert us from our purpose. Life's many challenges may find ways to disrupt our well-being, and suddenly, we may feel adrift in our quest for understanding.

Do not despise the difficulties you faced while trying to understand many things. If you ever find yourself in such a situation, you may need to go beyond simply being a good person. In an ordinary world, it's not easy to lose our way and rediscover our purpose. Therefore, be grateful to the Lord for guiding you back to reality once more. It's not an easy task to rediscover your purpose, especially when you've been disturbed by something that could have taken your entire essence away from you.

Perhaps you are someone who has inherited the title of being a human being. In that case, you have a responsibility to continue your family's legacy and live accordingly. If you were born into a world of scarcity and wish to succeed, you must transcend this level of existence and aspire to become something greater. Break through the barriers of understanding and step onto the platform where seemingly impossible achievements are within reach.

Believe in your potential to be extraordinary. Have faith that no matter how challenging or time-consuming a task may be, you possess the necessary knowledge and superior qualities to become more than you have ever been. Regardless of how daunting everything may seem, maintain confidence in your abilities and strive to be the best version of yourself.

Perhaps one day, your wishes will be granted, and you will be accepted for who you truly are. Your desire has always been to reach for the stars and bring your ultimate vision to life, all while fulfilling your responsibilities without fear. You are capable of achieving this. You can surpass the limitations of human understanding and become what many have never dared to be. Remember that we are not fated for grandeur; our destiny lies in making the most of what we have. However, if you reach for your star, you can truly become the person you are meant to be and attain all that you need for a lifetime.

Chapter Ten

I am the difference

What sets one person apart and makes them special compared to another person, even when they live in the same place and share similar interests, is that each individual perceives the world differently. Although deep down, we all have the desire to achieve success, the paths we choose to follow towards our goals can differ greatly. One person might decide to take a challenging route that many question, causing concern about whether they will succeed in their chosen journey.

At times, you may feel like you have no other option but to pursue this unique path, even though you could have chosen to be like everyone else. We all have the freedom to be whoever we want to be, but for some reason, you couldn't conform to the norm. Instead, you decided to pursue your own distinct path, which ultimately became your primary objective, giving meaning to your entire existence.

You discover yourself doing something you're deeply passionate about, unable to let go, while others continue with their lives in different ways, achieving success in line with their values. Occasionally, you might feel envious, wishing that time could synchronize for everyone so that you could all be on the same page. However, you recognize that you prioritize different aspects of life, and achieving that synchrony is an unattainable dream.

Following your passion can be fulfilling, but it may also result in falling behind in other important areas that matter in the short term. Despite our unwavering commitment to our chosen paths, we may encounter formidable obstacles that are difficult to overcome. This, in turn, can lead to deep feelings of despair, as we are, after all, human beings who respond to life's challenges in similar ways. During such moments, you may linger in uncertainty, hoping for a guiding light or a revelation that will illuminate the path you have selected.

Many factors motivate a person to pursue a particular path in life. It's not always about desires or what we lack; often, it's about addressing the unresolved issues in our own lives. Ultimately, the key to self-improvement lies in understanding ourselves and finding closure with our imperfections.

As we journey through life, each of us takes a unique route, cherishing our thoughts and occasionally making mistakes we believe we can easily correct. However, human beings are complex, and despite our best efforts, some things remain difficult to set right. Some aspects of our lives can be swiftly mended, while others prove stubbornly resistant, leading us down unexpected paths.

In such moments, we face a choice: either settle for a version of ourselves that doesn't truly reflect who we are, or believe that our aspirations will eventually align with our evolving selves as we navigate the journey of self-discovery and personal growth.

Sometimes, the obstacle isn't what we're pursuing, but rather our own internal struggles. We may become so focused on external achievements that we forget to nurture our inner selves. We yearn to see our dreams materialize, hoping to transform into the individuals we wish to be in society. Yet, we overlook the fact that our past, our true selves, can influence and shape our path in unexpected ways.

Initially, our motivation is simple—to be more, to make a meaningful impact, to feel alive.

We're all striving for something that allows us to truly be ourselves, where we can find contentment in our own skin. However, this isn't always an easy journey, and many of us carry this desire within us. Failing to achieve our goals can be especially disheartening when we bear sole responsibility for our destiny, leaving us with no one to blame but ourselves. Our aspiration is simple: we yearn for a path that unlocks our full potential and introduces us to the world. Yet, the creative journey is vast, diverse, and often burdensome, laden with the weight of our past.

Despite the potential for setbacks, we must cling to our ideas. We are individuals struggling to bring our deepest desires to life. Along this path, we steadfastly believe in the rightness of our aspirations, even when obstacles loom large. It's not a matter of not understanding; there are simply many constraints that bind us. Living life on our own terms, as we see it, can sometimes hinder progress until we find ourselves trapped, unsure of how to proceed, and yearning for normalcy once more.

What often happens is that we plunge headlong into our pursuits without fully considering that plans can go awry. As we become deeply committed, the challenges of the world become more apparent. Perhaps, at some point, you had a choice—you could have looked away, lived an ordinary life, and never worried about a thing. But now, you're fully immersed, and there's no turning back. Our very essence demands unwavering attention to our quest. We often fail to recognize how external factors can impact us negatively, choosing instead to focus on the beauty that can emerge if we succeed.

You might not always see the moments where you find yourself facing challenges. When life gets tough, you often discover your own unique path. This journey may lead you to confront difficult decisions that shape your character. When your future is in your hands, you may need to make precise choices in everything you undertake, requiring intense focus. Time is precious, especially when you didn't anticipate how your actions could hinder your progress for a while.

Our world is designed for people to live together harmoniously, with mechanisms in place to correct past mistakes, enabling us to progress normally. However, if you embark on a journey of self-discovery, your past may come back to haunt you. You may find it difficult to move forward like others, as your own intentions, meant to harm neither yourself nor anyone else, disrupt your life once more.

Our world is far from perfect, and we aren't born with all-encompassing knowledge of life's complexities. Daily mistakes influence the reality we hope to create. We seldom achieve the ideal vision; there's always something greater than us that shapes our perception of creation, leading to unmet expectations. If you lack unwavering faith deep within, you may stumble in your humble beginnings and give up too soon. However, if you maintain belief in your pursuits, regardless of the obstacles, a new beginning can dawn tomorrow.

If you summon the courage to take a step forward, you might find yourself embarking on a new path. This is what distinguishes us as individuals, our relentless hunger to see our own ideas come to life. In a typical society, human beings are driven by the desire to contribute to something greater than themselves, something that shapes their identity.

When we journey through life independently, we often encounter challenges that could make comprehending everything a bit challenging. Regrettably, we can't always correct yesterday's mistakes to create a brighter tomorrow, even with the knowledge we possess about our own lives.

At times, we might feel constrained by the pursuit of our aspirations. This limitation could arise from the decision to venture in our unique direction, effectively disconnecting ourselves from the protective shield of a predefined path. Now, your destiny rests solely in your hands, and the daily spark of rejuvenation may be absent, leaving you ensnared in your own creation. If you happen to lose sight of the right path, you may find yourself straying further into darkness, gradually losing touch with the meaningful aspects of life. As your own caretaker, the original influences that shaped you might not necessarily guide you along the correct course, resulting in a progressively shadowy journey.

In your pursuit of becoming the person you aspire to be, you might relinquish aspects of your former self. The more intensely you concentrate on your goals, the greater the responsibility you bear for your own development. Despite the need for personal experiences and knowledge, we must recognize that these are intrinsic to our essence. We don't always take pride in who we are, often facing challenging disappointments along the way. However, by nurturing a seed of love within ourselves, we can transform into something extraordinary. This transformation becomes a captivating narrative to share with the world, a vivid portrait to paint for all to behold.

At the end of the day, it's not like our past was a weakness. We had our own unique stories to share with the world. It's impossible to predict the truth about human emotions and foresee the future. Similarly, it's challenging to encapsulate someone's entire life. We possess our individuality, which serves as a canvas for creating art. Our life experiences weave together to craft the grand narrative that teaches humanity valuable lessons.

Our lives themselves are a form of creativity, the core of understanding that encompasses everything we've gone through, everything we are, and the love we hold in our hearts for our aspirations.

When we live our lives according to our vision and follow ordinary routines, we can learn from our daily mistakes. These mistakes may taint our past, but through our daily activities, we can easily move forward. On the contrary, art, a part of us, holds onto everything. To rediscover ourselves, we must revisit all that defines us and progress in the right direction. We nurture our essence with love, find the beauty in our actions, and discover angles that excite people. Sharing our stories effectively empowers us to overcome obstacles.

Sometimes, we may find ourselves trapped in situations with no apparent exit. We keep moving in circles without a clear way out. However, when we discover how to address our past experiences, we can move forward with new-found clarity. This transformation comes through embracing our past with love and evolving from it.

If you find it hard to understand yourself in both the worlds you live in, you may feel stuck, trying to find a solution or a way to make things better. In this situation, you may realize that you have no one to rely on but yourself because it's your life, and it's up to you to gain understanding. Without participating in any aspect of life's creation, you might never find a solution and remain trapped in your own world. Even though you may want to move forward, it seems impossible, and you'll feel stuck forever.

By engaging in any form of participation, which can be seen as an art within us, we give ourselves a second chance to correct our past mistakes and do things right. So, if you aspire to become a true artist, you must grasp everything related to your own life. Even in situations where you didn't fully understand, you can find a way to address potential problems.

With dedication, we can transform any situation until we uncover the love within it, even if we've been inadequate in various ways. When you contemplate changing your life and making things right, you might need to discover something that excites you and can serve as the path you follow. Identifying your own talents can provide an opportunity to overcome difficult situations and setbacks encountered on the journey of creation.

Although you might have traveled a path free of regrets, where no rectifications are necessary, and no effort is needed to set things right in your life, you may find it lacking in motivation. This lack of participation may have caused your world to become isolated. Now, you must rely on your own understanding, and there's no one to blame but yourself. You also have no one to guide you out of this situation except yourself. Your well-being depends on your own abilities to achieve success, and you must strive for excellence regardless of how many are focused on their own paths.

Within each of us resides a unique artistic essence waiting to be discovered. You have the choice to embrace this hidden talent or turn a blind eye to it forever. This process is an integral part of resolving the challenges we previously couldn't foresee in our journey towards self-realization.

Understanding your path towards your dreams and future success involves acknowledging and addressing the setbacks you've encountered along the way. These hurdles, once faced, become an inextricable part of your identity, and some aspects of your being may require reconstruction to align with reality.

Even when you attempt to distance yourself from your past self, there are times when you must revisit those memories. Some individuals inherently possess an artistic flair and are compelled to share their stories, while others find their purpose in forging ahead relentlessly.

When you have a world of opportunities before you, you may be called upon to confront challenging situations. Clarity brings relief from suffering, and all the elements needed for your personal narrative - characters, plot, and protagonist - are already within you. To dispel the grip of these inner struggles, you must open up to those around you, and equilibrium will be restored.

Consider the impact of events, for they affect each of us uniquely. Perhaps it was you who bore the brunt of adversity. Others may have navigated life's challenges more smoothly, suffering less loss than you. Every event, while observable by all, wields a distinctive influence on our individual journeys. You may find yourself deeply scarred by an experience that left a lasting mark.

Ultimately, it falls upon you to revisit those moments and embark on a journey of healing and self-restoration, mending the wounds that have afflicted you along the way.

While we gain valuable lessons from our past experiences, which we consider essential for life, there are moments when we face challenging situations that are hard to justify. In certain circumstances, there will always be a part of you that doesn't fully comprehend what happened; it feels as though numerous obstacles hindered your well-being. It can seem as if a series of unfortunate events intentionally conspired to cause you harm. When you reflect on who you've become, it's evident that these setbacks have somehow impeded your progress. Even if you wished to move forward, you find it challenging to live with the lingering repercussions. Now, you must revisit those circumstances and find a way to transform them. Our identity is shaped by the trials and tribulations we encounter in life, and ignoring these experiences means overlooking a crucial part of yourself. Achieving your full potential becomes difficult under such circumstances.

For a brief moment, you may have been unable to envision how everything would fit into the grand scheme of your future. Even if you were to forgive yourself for past mistakes, it doesn't make everything right or align with the person you aspire to be. It might have been a phase in your life that you traversed, but there's a part of you that requires personal effort to achieve closure and contentment. When you confront and overcome these challenges, you'll realize that nothing was ever meant to harm you, and you're not facing rejection. Instead, you're given an opportunity to rectify your former self and chart a new path for yourself.

At times, we're not presented with the achievements we've earned but rather with the chance to rectify our wrongs. In the midst of this, you've chosen to embrace your humanity, embodying someone who values self-reliance and holds onto their identity. While some things may need to be forgotten, certain aspects of our past will inevitably catch up with us if we haven't resolved them thoroughly. For an extended period, you may find it challenging to figure out how to mend that particular part of your life.

We often receive the wrongs we've gathered in life, even more than we think we deserve. We sometimes miss chances to do good, which is a part of ourselves we cherish. But living with numerous mistakes can be tough. That's why we're offered a second opportunity to correct our errors through the power of art. It might seem unnecessary to ignore these opportunities. So, what happens to those who fail to look back and fix their past mistakes? Where do they end up?

As we work hard to make things right in our lives, perhaps some people have nothing to rectify. Maybe art is a way for someone to live and share their story with others. Most people have the freedom to be whatever they choose to be. They absorb the pain and gain a better understanding of themselves. They realize their capability to do things correctly. They're entrusted with responsibilities they must use for the greater good. They must transform situations or make amends so that everyone can live happily ever after.

We all exist on the same level, part of the reality, and together we create a meaningful story about existence. Each of us plays a role. Those whose lives are dedicated to creativity become the bearers of pain. They write about it for others to understand and derive good from their suffering. They bring out the darkest aspects of their souls, casting away the darkness in our lives to reveal the light in the world.

For those who live to tell stories, finding meaning in life requires interpreting what they've seen. This is as important as what others do to move forward in the world. What if there's something vital you must share with the world, but no one wants to take the spotlight? What becomes of you in this creative process? You become a significant missing piece in the universe, disrupting people from fully embracing themselves because you refuse to share your own story.

Who helps fix your role when we, as humanity, suffer from your actions? What happens to those who don't take responsibility for what they do? Now, we seek relief from the consequences of your deeds, as they cause us pain. Maybe it's not our main concern, as we all have our own battles. Inside every person, there's a darkness we must fight to set free our true selves.

No matter who you are, you must overcome this darkness in your life, or it can trap you and affect your daily life and relationships. We all know where we've fallen short of our ideals or struggled to move forward, and now we're left disappointed with the world.

Art allows us to reflect on ourselves and find solutions to past mistakes, improving the present and shaping a better future. When you feel stuck and surrounded by darkness, it seems like everything is against you. You may try your best, but it feels like your efforts are in vain. However, conquering this setback can lead to a fresh start and a brighter future.

It's like a thief that strikes at night, taking away everything you've saved and earned. No matter how hard you work, it seems to vanish, and it keeps consuming you.

By dedicating ourselves to the world of art, we can revisit moments and chapters in our lives where we failed to do things properly. These moments can eventually become the ties that connect us to nothingness, offering us an opportunity to reclaim what rightfully belongs to us. You may have lived while complaining about the thief who continually steals from your life, but this thievery didn't start recently. It began a long time ago, gradually taking away everything of value in your current existence—love, family, money, and happiness, leaving you with little more than sorrow.

Yet, if we aspire to attain success, we must exert significant effort to gain a deeper understanding of life. We must diligently work to create a level of excellence based on faith, surpassing all weaknesses and setbacks, propelling us toward a brighter tomorrow. Once you have wholeheartedly committed yourself, even without comprehending how it transpired, and after confronting the light and dark aspects of your entire being, you may begin to witness the emergence of a new day.

You will find satisfaction in knowing that your relentless pursuit of perfection has allowed you to construct a legacy around the things you hold most dear. It is clear that many may struggle to bring an idea to fruition and ultimately give up. However, you, who persist with unwavering belief until your thoughts materialize, have triumphed over your fears.

We create our legacy through both joyful moments and challenging times. We confront the formidable adversary that threatens to seize all that we hold dear. When we emerge victorious from the darkest of circumstances and navigate our way through sorrowful experiences, we learn how to become our unique selves. This adversary could be anything that has shattered the things closest to our hearts, deeply ingrained in our very essence. As a result, we find ourselves living a life devoid of happiness and enjoyment. It might be something that has deprived us of any opportunity for self-expression, leaving us wondering how we can retain our humanity when this relentless thief seeks to pilfer everything we treasure.

In the wake of such a loss, we are denied both peace and the chance to love, casting a long shadow over the rest of our lives. The absence of all that sustains us, including someone to tend to our needs, leaves us questioning its whereabouts. We ponder what we once were, what we are now, and what is rightfully ours. Deep within us, we acknowledge the extent of the damage, aware that nothing can surpass the harm already inflicted. We know precisely where it has wounded us and how it has shaped our experiences. This menacing force threatens our well-being, determined to strip us of all that we hold dear. Failing to emerge victorious in this battle means never achieving our most cherished desires.

This malevolent presence in our lives hungers for everything we possess, showing no intention of departing any time soon. Finding a solution in a single day is improbable. Nevertheless, if we are fully prepared for success, we can prevail over this challenge, even though circumstances may persistently attempt to return us to our starting point or ignite our frustrations. Yet, once we uncover our love for creation and creativity within, we possess the power to transform every aspect of life into a work of art.

At some point in life, we all reach a moment where we must discover our true selves and embrace the reality we wish to celebrate. It's important to recognize that our essence should never be taken from us, forever stolen by negative forces like thieves, criminals, or elements that don't belong in our world. We must summon our inner strength to resist anything that aims to harm what matters most to us. Without realization, we might wake up to a brighter day. In the midst of questioning why life has dealt us certain challenges, we can eventually find peace by facing and addressing what lies ahead.

Confronting the challenges in our lives is a path chosen by those who aspire to make the most of their current existence. While it's natural to wish for someone to rescue and heal us from difficult situations, we all have our own individual battles to wage. No one else can stand up to and overcome your setbacks for you. Each person faces their unique hurdles as they strive to achieve their desires in this world. Ultimately, those who turn away and avoid confronting their obstacles continue to live the same monotonous lives filled with sorrow.

On the flip side, those who never waver become the architects of their destinies, building a strong and enduring foundation. The metaphorical 'beast' represents the challenges that obstruct your path in this lifetime, preventing you from realizing your dreams. If you don't overcome these obstacles, they will multiply, grow stronger, and threaten everything you hold dear. Your struggles will persist from one generation to the next, affecting your descendants long after you've passed away.

So, you discover a meaningful purpose to dedicate your efforts to, where everything you have to offer finds its place. As you journey towards your goal's fulfillment, you come to realize that the time and energy invested have not been in vain. You've devoted yourself to a cause that makes life worth living, and despite potential setbacks today, your dedication to doing things right offers the promise of future victories, leading to everlasting happiness. This fulfillment isn't just for your own benefit; it extends to future generations as well.

While you might have started with very little to hold onto, you've learned to cling to this idea, granting you the opportunity to start anew. These struggles didn't originate with your generation; they've been ongoing battles, faced by your parents, grandparents, and ancestors before them. Regrettably, you might be encountering the same challenges, and those who come after you may endure them too. Had they succeeded, it would have spared us from these physical and challenging conflicts. Those who inherited the gift of life instead of these enduring wars are fortunate.

It's unfortunate that each of us has a role to play, and our abilities vary. Perhaps you've entertained the notion that you might be an exception, capable of succeeding by chance alone. However, you can never truly understand someone else's inner strength. Those who have glimpsed the other side have conquered their fears, while you wonder why you remain entangled in a system that seems impossible to escape. The formidable adversary has set its sights on you, seeking to extinguish the radiant star within you, ready to obliterate everything you hold dear. The curse can only be broken when you unearth the power to change lives. You will labor tirelessly until you unleash your inner potential, reaching for your deepest talents and becoming the person you've always aspired to be.

Discovering the meaning within the overflow of your emotions, because that truly reflects your essence, and you never accepted anything less than your true worth. Devoting yourself completely and conquering the inner demons that threatened your existence, leaving your former self behind. Defying the inevitability of human mortality, and letting go of all preconceived notions about you, never to be bound by any spell again. You shine like a star, destined to return to the very core of creation. Your existence will never be on the same plane; the dust that once shaped you, like everyone else, returns to its origins.

For those who have waged lifelong battles, triumphing over every challenge and conquering their innermost fears, what awaits them at the end? They embark on a journey of free will, creating their own constellation where they eternally unite with the wellspring of creation. Despite our diverse perspectives and individuality, what happens when we reach that destination? Do we all merge into a new form of existence, working not just for ourselves but for the collective? How can one manage the multitude of lives, each with its own path, and still face common struggles if we falter? It's true that some must focus on the present, recognizing that not everyone can remain behind. Each plays their unique role, and the one who emerges victorious does so for the benefit of all.

Art plays a crucial role in shaping our new lives. It unlocks opportunities to explore uncharted territories, offering strength in our ongoing struggles. Our pursuit of understanding enables us to craft a new world, a vision we aim to manifest. Amidst all this, remember, you are not confined; you stand out not only within your community and circle of friends but also possess a unique essence that goes deeper.

Your impact resonates most profoundly within your family, where your presence is invaluable. You bring hope to countless lives and persistently seek solutions to the challenges obstructing your path. We illuminate our world because your actions can ripple through, and adversities can leave lasting marks on your spirit.

The battles within your home are reflections of universal struggles and creation itself. You have the potential to be your true self, and yet, a single family's dynamics can affect the entire world. You hold the power to rectify this, standing firm as a voice for those you represent, striving to make a positive impact in this lifetime. Your influence transcends ordinary goodness, reaching a realm where many can find contentment within themselves.

Not all hardships or delays are intended to harm you. Some delays serve as stepping stones, enabling you to construct a legacy essential for your happiness.

Embrace your uniqueness, no matter how different you may be. Always remember that there is something responsible for all the wrongs in your life. Even the moments when you felt trapped, like you were stuck in a never-ending cycle. All the challenges you face are somehow connected, stemming from a common source of negativity. Stand firm against these obstacles that try to steal your happiness. Conquer those inner fears, and persist until you reach the point where your potential shines brilliantly.

You are a one-of-a-kind individual, and your creativity is what sets you apart from the crowd. It's the force that brings your true self to the surface, and it will never let you down, even if you have to put certain aspects of your life on hold as you pursue your dreams. The reality is, things could remain stagnant until you discover that unique essence within you, destined for greatness and meant to conquer all challenges.

Don't allow anything to permanently steal your joy. If you desire change, your creativity is the guiding light that can help you overcome the challenges in your life. It can also empower you to excel in any aspect of your life, whether it's within your family or on a global scale. Your creativity is a reflection of your beliefs, and you don't have to be a genius to express yourself through it. It's there to embody what you stand for and share your unique message with the world.

Chapter Eleven

If I answered prayers

Doing something correctly doesn't always revolve around personal desires or financial gain. It's important to consider how your actions affect others who will become part of your endeavor. Our actions have a profound impact on people in various ways, and we can't predict how they'll be received by those around us. Having the ability to make a positive impact on others is a rare quality that isn't frequently encountered in the world. Human beings yearn for love and connection, and it's crucial to ensure that you're contributing positively to the world.

Defining the purpose of your existence without showing care for the lives of others is a difficult task. Who can better spread a message of hope and companionship than you? Waiting for someone else to take action isn't a productive approach. What would you have achieved in your life if you simply waited for things to fall into place? It's essential to take initiative and not sit idly by, hoping for someone else to fulfill a certain role you've neglected.

While we may not be perfect and can't do everything, we must have faith that our efforts, no matter how eager we are to succeed, are sufficient for both ourselves and others. However, the nagging question of how to justify our lives remains. How can you claim to have fulfilled your purpose if you haven't strived

"

to be the best version of yourself? Under normal circumstances, we shouldn't compromise our lives. At some point, we must do something extraordinary that brings out our true potential, even in challenging circumstances where we have limited understanding.

We are all born with free will, minds, and hearts, and we should use these gifts to do good in the world. Our actions define us, and we may only have one chance to make a lasting impression on others. In a world filled with challenges and negativity, we must make an effort to show that we care about others. This is what gives meaning to our lives, without diminishing anyone else's worth. We don't need to change who we are; we just need to find a way to share our unique qualities with the world. Authentic love for ourselves becomes a powerful force that draws people from all walks of life towards us, helping them understand us better.

Unfortunately, not everyone seizes the opportunity that life presents to them. It's not others who suffer from our uniqueness; it's often ourselves struggling to find contentment. Periodically, we must advocate for who we are, and if there is no love or care in our actions, we are essentially justifying the person we've become.

There's nothing wrong with wanting to be known for something remarkable. Our efforts should aim to exemplify the qualities that people want to associate with. We must find effective ways to share our lives with others and collaborate harmoniously with them until they fully understand our essence. By allowing others to experience the world through our perspective, we can bring them closer to self-discovery, even in the face of adversity. Your journey might not have been easy, but in the end, you were able to achieve your objectives, making it all worthwhile.

What people desire most is to have someone who can accompany them throughout their entire life, no matter what challenges they encounter. This person could be there for them in various aspects, like relationships, family matters, finances, or general life experiences. They provide the much-needed support during tough times, offering a boost to self-esteem and guiding them toward a better path. Even if they're not present all the time, they seize the chance to uplift and empower. Without delving into the diverse paths we traverse, it's clear that our character is molded by such situations.

We may not always pinpoint the exact moment we embarked on our personal journeys, but somewhere along the way, there was a catalyst that transformed us into who we are today. We must recognize that we aren't solely shaped by formal education or external influences; it's our inner spirit, our profound essence, that yearns to explore the world, seek more, and embrace new experiences. This inner drive becomes the path we tread.

Regrettably, we only have one opportunity to define our identity, and once we commit, it's challenging to abandon these deeply ingrained beliefs. Your choice can potentially shape your entire life, with no easy escape from the consequences of your decision. Before you solidify your identity, carefully consider your choices; you won't easily alter your course later and may rue the path that led you to your current state.

Even at a young age, you may find yourself confronted with mature, weighty decisions, often without the chance for a course correction. It's not that our actions are intended to harm others, but the choices we make, whether intentionally or unintentionally, can significantly influence our future selves.

We must acknowledge that the outcomes in our lives are akin to seeds sown within us; whatever we plant will flourish. Whether it's a habitual behavior we've adopted or an unexpected choice we've made, it all has roots somewhere. Realize that each wise decision you make is like sowing a seed in your heart.

Perhaps your journey didn't commence on a positive note, and for much of your life, you may have neglected your responsibilities. This oversight won't go unnoticed; it has a way of infiltrating your daily life and stunting your progress. You come to realize the importance of consistently making sound, courageous decisions, even when they're not easy. These choices ultimately shape your future. It's astonishing to see that the fruits you're now enjoying are the result of seeds sown long ago. This teaches us a valuable lesson about life.

It's disheartening to acknowledge that some aspects of who you've become cannot be permanently undone. If your past has been marked by disappointments, it might seem like life lacks purpose. However, now that you understand how our lives take shape, can you look away? Regardless of your circumstances, strive to do good so that goodness may find its way back to you.

It becomes evident that we must consider our life's path carefully. We can choose to drift aimlessly, or we can make a deliberate choice to pursue what we're most passionate about. Something that sets us apart and makes us unique. Once you make that choice, you'll embark on a journey towards success.

How many different paths can we choose in life? But to truly succeed, shouldn't our lives have something extraordinary? Indeed, to experience goodness in our daily lives, we may need to start walking down the path that leads to our deepest desires. You'll be amazed by how much you can achieve, simply by sowing the right seeds in your heart.

While some things can't last forever, it's important to continually do good deeds and strive for greatness in the paths we've chosen. Yet, don't hesitate to do something unique once in a while, something that won't fade away, an idea whose value remains constant, whether for better or worse. Ask yourself, what kind of work endures? What can withstand the test of time, even in a fast-paced world—an invention that retains its significance? And what kind of dedication is required for such lasting worth?

We must work hard, knowing that over time, things can deteriorate and lose their value. New opportunities emerge, and we may seem less important. But if people are at the heart of everything you do, much of your significance will endure. When things go wrong, humanity will remember how you dedicated yourself to making a difference. While it's not easy to achieve, determination and the desire to do good can elevate you to such a level.

This is what touches many lives—a life lived with good intentions and a desire to benefit others. It's about caring and taking action without needing prompting, creating something remarkable for people to celebrate. When you refuse to turn away from the truth, you become part of the solution, not just for personal gain but for the love of humanity.

There are always opportunities to lend a hand, but sometimes greed blinds us as we seek excessive benefits. We view everything as a business opportunity and invest our lives in it, craving more. When it becomes difficult to profit easily, we persist stubbornly.

No matter what we do, if it's something meant to last longer than usual, we might need to pay extra attention compared to ordinary situations. Sometimes, we might even forget that we aim to benefit from such an endeavor. This isn't easy because our actions are always driven by the desire to earn a living. Achieving both things simultaneously, as we had hoped, can be challenging. It may require us to transform our deepest goal into the journey of our life. We should allow it to take over our entire existence, making it the focal point of who we are. We should commit ourselves to positively impacting lives in every possible way, and the rewards will follow.

Understanding why there's a need to reach a level where we embody true love for humanity might be difficult. Nevertheless, this could be our way of responding to people's prayers. Humans have many things they wish to accomplish in their lives, and the path to reaching them may revolve around prioritizing care. We offer the love in our hearts, even though dealing with daily challenges can be demanding because it's a lifelong dedication. Living with the knowledge that deep in our hearts, we gave ourselves to a noble cause, and much of that journey wasn't about us, but rather, the well-being of others.

In the end, it's not that we won't benefit from what we're doing; we will. However, to enjoy long-lasting benefits, we may need to give more of ourselves than the average person. It becomes a lifetime commitment to caring for those who need us in their lives, with the ambition of making their well-being the core of our actions. Sometimes, what truly matters is knowing that we're adding value, and that's more significant than living without purpose.

It's essential to cherish the idea we hold in our hearts, especially for those who've seen the positive impact of hard work in their lives. We may need to work diligently without worrying about when success will arrive because continuous effort might be necessary to maximize our gains in life. We must take a leap of faith, believing that tomorrow will be better, and our desires will eventually be fulfilled.

Caring for the world and those around us is crucial, and you have the power to do good deeds that help people discover their true selves. People might eventually realize that even when things seem complicated, positive changes are possible. Despite the universe's vast complexity, in our everyday lives, there's an ongoing need for better ways of doing things. This need is insatiable, no matter how fast our lives may appear. Love will always be a fundamental necessity, no need to endlessly search for what's missing in this world and how to benefit from it.

The answers you seek have always existed, stemming from your inherent need for life, the questions, and prayers that have been with you since the beginning of time. By dedicating yourself to such devotion, you might forget past neglect and create something beautiful through your understanding. When we shoulder responsibilities, we not only become valuable human beings but also gain personal fulfillment. Many fail to realize their true selves, and you can help them understand who they truly are by navigating these situations.

If you commit to enduring responsibilities, your existence will be everlasting, and your contributions to this world will be remembered. Your dedication, whatever it may be, will eventually manifest its significance, even if it doesn't seem evident now. It's essential to recognize that when these responsibilities vanish, your importance diminishes. We start our lives as responsibilities to our parents and other parties, seeking worth and contentment through our responsibilities.

As we grow, we take on new obligations through parenting and our intellectual pursuits. When children grow up or the tasks we once prioritized lose their relevance, our lives can become uncertain. While you may have children or others to care for, it's essential to find a deeper purpose from within your heart to remain focused and connected to the broader fabric of existence. In doing so, your existence remains secure, and it goes beyond the mere pursuit of wealth or personal benefits. It's about creating lasting value and a meaningful legacy. As we age, we must recognize that evolving into a responsible, purpose-driven human being is key to serving a noble and enduring objective.

We make choices about how we want to live our lives. One option is to strive for something meaningful, something that will make you memorable forever. Another choice is to simply exist without purpose. It's important to realize that everything you need has always been within you; there's no need to search for it externally.

Sometimes, it may be unclear why you need to focus deeply. However, the secret may lie in the process of delving deeper into understanding. Through this journey, you can reach a level of profound knowledge about creation. Creativity requires dedication; to stand out as an individual, you must put in the effort to see your ideas flourish. If you achieve what you desire, you will enjoy the lasting rewards of your hard work.

The path to realizing your dreams may involve sacrifices, and unexpected challenges can arise along the way, testing your resilience. It may feel like the universe is conspiring against you, but success demands an understanding of the choices you made to become who you are. We often fear pursuing our true desires, observing others achieve their dreams without realizing they put in their own effort at some point. We must remember that we also have a role to play in our journey.

Sometimes, you might doubt your abilities and believe your mind is insufficient for a certain task. However, upon introspection, you may find that there's no easy path to being comfortable with the person you've become. The truth is, you're not weak or inadequate for pursuing your passions. Expressing the value of your pursuits can be challenging, and conveying what's happening inside your mind is no simple task.

Considering the multitude of activities we engage in, it's possible that the way you experience things is unique to you. The path you're currently on isn't necessarily incorrect; it's your journey to resolve your own challenges. However, it's important to realize that there isn't always a straightforward route to what appears right. Somewhere along this journey, before everything falls into place, it's crucial to acknowledge that you haven't been left behind. Much of what you're doing is part of your personal growth.

As you continue on this path, you're progressing toward a better direction, and there's a rewarding outcome that awaits you at the end of each day. You are recognized for leading the way and approaching tasks correctly. Your confidence and intelligence grow, and while it may seem like everyone achieves similar results, it's not always the case. Sometimes, it's about doing things correctly. It boils down to excelling in everything you do while remaining true to yourself, reflecting your character, and indicating whether you value who you are and prioritize your well-being.

Even if you're not the absolute best, or maybe you don't possess the most remarkable ideas, it's crucial to engage in activities that define your individuality or indulge in your greatest passions. Achieving our desired goals may not always be straightforward, as we tend to assess our abilities based on our current circumstances. Despite the apparent ease of our current situation, we may encounter limitations along our journey. We are, after all, limited by our natural progression. Youth is fleeting, and this might be one of the most challenging lessons in the creative process.

Over time, you may find it increasingly difficult to acquire certain skills that set you apart. Consider that developing the ability to carefully analyze ideas and ensure their logical coherence is a skill that requires dedicated practice from an early stage.

It's not a matter of whether you possess innate talent or not. As age catches up with us, we often grapple with introspective questions, attempting to determine the true nature of our actions – are they virtuous or flawed? These answers can sow seeds of doubt in our hearts, especially when we fail to witness the fruits of our labor materialize, leaving us in a state of perpetual uncertainty and seeking closure.

When you pay close attention to what other people are doing, you might not be able to achieve what you really want. Instead of following someone else's path, try to understand your true desires better. This way, you can get closer to your destiny. Always remember that to make a significant impact, you should think of it as planting a seed, nurturing it with the love in your heart, and waiting for it to bear fruit.

Imagine a tree grown from genuine knowledge and understanding, a tree that no one can ever cut down. Consider what you can accomplish by valuing your unique self. Don't pretend to be someone you're not; embrace your true self. Remember, it's not about where you started; it's about what you decide to do with your journey.

Now, while some things from your past can't be changed, you can't go back to the easy days of youth, you have today, tomorrow, and a lifetime ahead to shape a better future. The present moment holds immense potential; you can embark on incredible endeavors that lead you to a more fulfilling life. Even if your past haunts you, eventually, you'll forget the person you used to be.

We bestow blessings upon fellow humans in numerous ways, granting them the freedom to shape their lives according to their desires. It is entirely within your power to opt for a path where you prioritize your own contentment above all else. Nevertheless, if you persist in such a manner, uncertainties will persistently infiltrate your heart, resulting in a state of feeling lost and uncertain about the objectives you seek to attain. These kinds of errors can exact a significant toll over time, even though there are ample opportunities to rectify our missteps on a daily basis, as all our actions serve the greater good.

There may come a day when you no longer have the opportunity to rectify your mistakes or undo your missteps. People extend numerous opportunities to us, provided we approach our endeavors with love and dedication. Many of the wrongs we commit can eventually be forgiven, granting us a fresh start. Each new day presents the potential to reinvent ourselves, and if you wish to witness your true potential unfold, you must steadfastly pursue your goals without questioning the necessity of dedicating yourself to this purpose.

We are human because we harbor aspirations we strive to realize, and without the drive to reach our objectives, life loses its sense of purpose. Somewhere deep within, you recognize that you deserve better, and this can only be achieved by fostering positivity in the lives of others.

True glory emerges from serving others, rewarding us with a precious gift that would remain elusive if pursued in isolation. Through our collective efforts in assisting fellow humans, we obtain something invaluable that money cannot purchase. These are the aspects of life, relationships, and the pursuit of truth that one should never compromise. The goodness of this world is fragile, and it is impossible to predict what may diminish it, or whom you may come to cherish.

Finding someone special who brings love, peace, harmony, and lasting happiness into your life is rare. Such individuals don't cross your path every day. It requires courage and dedication to attract someone truly remarkable into your daily existence. Relationships can be complex and challenging. It's difficult to know the depths of someone's love because it often unfolds behind closed doors without any witnesses.

Ultimately, we learn to tolerate each other, for the human experience is not meant to be lived in solitude. A good heart tends to attract what it embodies. Nonetheless, taking a stand and striving for greatness is essential if you want to leave a lasting legacy. Perhaps it's your responsibility to contribute greatly to humanity, as people yearn for heroes who selflessly work towards shared goals.

You may wonder why you aren't the one in need of someone's sacrifice, but the answer lies in embracing your humanity and experiencing a life that many can only dream of. So, how should you lead your life? By dedicating yourself to a purpose that positively impacts countless lives, helping them discover their full potential. In a world that often feels bleak, you can be the source of hope, turning dreams into reality and fostering enduring happiness.

If this is what truly matters to you, then go beyond the ordinary and embark on a journey that few may comprehend. Walk alongside others, overcoming the obstacles that have hindered their progress, and together, reach for greatness and glory.

Chapter Twelve

Confident

To reach a point where we fully grasp the art of generating our own innovative concepts, we embark on a journey of self-discovery and view the act of creation with fresh perspective. We must temporarily set aside our current human existence and concentrate on aspiring to become someone of significance, aligning with our deepest aspirations. This process often commences in the initial stages of our creative thought process, where we may cling to our past identities, origins, and possessions. This inner attachment can both hinder and confine us, diverting our focus from our true selves. As long as this internal struggle persists, we remain subject to a pervasive human phenomenon that opposes our most cherished desires.

Our existence is driven by the pursuit of something greater than our present selves. If you still see yourself as the same person you were yesterday, you may not be succeeding as you could be; you have yet to transcend self-limitation and attain success. However, upon introspection, you may discover a unique individual within, beckoned by a higher calling, eager to explore the realm of creation. Rather than remaining trapped in a world that seeks to diminish your worth and marginalize you, you have broken through the gates of self-imposed limitations, recognizing your true value.

The past version of yourself that once stood before you has vanished, and you have emerged as a new individual—one who acknowledges an innate, exceptional quality within. This love for yourself has empowered you, preparing you for the challenges of the world. You have come to comprehend your profound fortune, realizing that you were not born at this elevated level and that destiny has placed you on this grand stage.

You emerged from humble beginnings, brimming with unwavering faith because you recognize that you possess a rare and exceptional talent, a gift you are eager to share with the world. When the opportunity arises, ensure you don't disappoint others. Reveal your true self and never allow anyone to limit your abilities or make you doubt your potential for greatness. You don't need others to define you because you've lived with the knowledge of who you are every day. The pain of being unique is a burden you carry, but you've embraced it. Your purpose is to embody your true self, showcasing your abilities and knowledge.

As you achieve the goals you once struggled to attain, don't cling to your past self. Embrace this new version of you and let go of your old identity, embracing the differences that make you stand out. This includes recognizing that you are meant to be something extraordinary, a shining example of true talent. When the world calls upon your inner essence, you respond by bringing forth your full potential to create a lasting impact. You, as a star, are filled with boundless talents, and that's what truly matters – a delightful surprise hidden within you.

Your journey to become what you truly desire has transformed you into a unique and exceptional individual. Through relentless dedication and hard work, you've risen from nothing to transcend common understanding and stand out. Therefore, as you strive for further greatness, don't merely hold onto a sliver of faith; dedicate your entire being to your ambitions. While we all have different roles to play in this world, yours speaks volumes about who you are and what you represent, deserving admiration.

We all shine as stars for various reasons, whether it's our appearance or our unique abilities. Some people harness the power of their looks to make a difference, and that's their role to fulfill. Their physical appearance is their extraordinary talent, setting them apart and captivating the world.

If you don't act in the right way, your attitude can affect your goals. When you doubt your abilities, you lose confidence, and you don't shine as brightly as you could. This means your belief in yourself isn't at its best, and you're not fully embracing your inner passion. You may undervalue yourself, disguising your true essence and how you see the world, how you understand who you are, and your perspective on life itself.

This is how we influence situations and the people around us to follow our lead, and that's enough to justify our commitment and efforts. When you deviate from your true path, you disappoint yourself, leading to inner struggles for self-acceptance. You can't fake who you are or your life experiences. Instead of dwelling on what's missing, focus on your genuine abilities.

Even if we have faced hardships and aspects of ourselves we dislike, we aim to make positive changes in our lives. Finding a platform to share our message with the world can help us overcome challenges. No matter how powerful our inner doubts may seem, the universe, in which we exist like stars, strengthens our ability to think freely and empowers us to overcome setbacks.

Many challenges we encounter may seem insurmountable, causing us to struggle with our thoughts. You might have spent years grappling with weaknesses that have now imprisoned you. Meanwhile, there is much you may not have truly appreciated, because you didn't know how to succeed with your understanding.

Therefore, do not allow things that you cannot reverse to change who you are. Never let anyone push you to the edge of life, attempting to make you think less of yourself. Negative obstacles may appear that threaten your well-being, particularly in your pursuit of numerous goals. These obstacles will persist as you journey through the path of creation. However, do not display fear or doubt your abilities. Stand firm for everything you believe in, which has found a place within you.

Various challenges may target you, and when faced with things you do not comprehend, appearing weak will only make matters worse. These challenges will continually exert pressure to bring you down. Therefore, it's crucial to exude confidence. This positive mindset acts as a protective shield in your life. When you finally break through to the other side, whatever problems you've faced will ultimately crumble.

Although the path to success in the vast world of stars may seem challenging and daunting, it's important to recognize that this journey is not for the faint of heart. It requires a high level of determination and resilience, qualities that are possessed by exceptionally strong individuals. These individuals not only persistently pursue their aspirations but also draw strength from the challenges they've faced. Instead of succumbing to setbacks, they rise above them and create something that truly reflects their inner strength.

Their journey isn't solely defined by the trials they've endured; it's also fueled by their unwavering optimism and their refusal to let circumstances dictate their life's course. They carry a profound sense of hope, which they aim to share with the world, and they possess the courage to stand up against anything that threatens to extinguish the flame of love burning within their souls.

In life, various circumstances can dampen our love and enthusiasm for everything around us. As human beings, it's imperative that we learn to overcome such challenges and emerge as shining stars, demonstrating to the world that triumph is indeed possible. Our purpose is to inspire hope in others, encouraging them to confront their fears with courage. We understand that as long as someone else is still grappling with the same setbacks we've faced or the adversities we've conquered, our victory isn't complete.

To overcome the inner battles within your soul is to triumph for the benefit of all. By ensuring you shine as a guiding light in your existence, you inspire others. When people gaze upon you, they see the potential for positive change. If these struggles persist, not only do others suffer, but you also deviate from your true self, and these challenges continue to plague your life. Sometimes, you may wonder why these situations keep happening to you. Remember, it's not just about you; many others face similar difficulties.

While we can't completely transform the world, we can set a high standard for those seeking guidance and personal growth. Whatever your pursuits may be, venture forth to inspire and motivate. This helps people comprehend you better amidst the complexities of reality, fostering courage in many to become better versions of themselves.

Especially for those eager to change, offer them the encouragement they seek. Sometimes, hearing what they want is all that matters. Doing so allows you to share messages of hope and prepares you for the day when opportunities arise. Showcase your abilities, as it's not that we lack the power to gain recognition; we often aren't adequately prepared for our deepest desires. When you're fully prepared, the world will welcome you with open arms.

At some point in life, you must make a decision about who you want to become. This choice will serve as your tool to navigate through the challenges of life. Being well-prepared for this chosen path is how we can become content with ourselves. People who persistently pursue their passions and interests, selecting them from among countless options in the world, often stand out as stars. They are human beings who are defined by their unique goals and aspirations.

This sense of purpose is what gives our lives meaning when we eventually reach the end. It allows us to live happily ever after, knowing that we have made something meaningful out of the things we have known throughout our lives. It's interesting how life unfolds as we make choices and work hard to succeed in our chosen paths. Perhaps your chosen path didn't seem promising from the beginning, and for a while, you had to struggle to perfect and understand what you were doing. However, with unwavering dedication, you managed to triumph over those challenges.

Don't deceive yourself into thinking that things will start making sense along the way without a clear direction. The clarity must be present from the very beginning when you choose the kind of life you want to lead. You gain profound experiences when you have a well-defined and solid idea to guide you. Many aspects of life only begin to make sense when you have such clarity. These are the qualities we should aim to embody. If our thoughts are not channeled through a path we are certain of, they may not significantly impact our journey.

You start by coming up with a new idea, and then you work on it tirelessly until it's absolutely perfect. As you do this, you also change and adapt to it until it becomes a fundamental part of your life. This transformation is what turns ordinary individuals into extraordinary stars. We become strong by pursuing our deepest desires to such an extent that they become our way of life, exactly as we envisioned it as a human being.

Along the way, you'll face numerous challenges, but if you don't have a strong belief in what you're doing, you won't make much progress. The first step is to discover your passion, and once you've found it, you must hold onto it, no matter how easy or difficult the journey becomes. These challenges often become the obstacles that shape us and guide us towards our desired destination. Failure becomes almost impossible when your purpose becomes an integral part of your daily life.

This approach defines our daily well-being as we continue on our creative journey. Many people fail because they lack clear goals along their path. Throughout the journey, you may encounter unexpected setbacks or delays, but eventually, everything aligns with what you truly need. It might not happen precisely when you want it or when you're in dire straits, but in the end, your reality conforms to your aspirations.

No matter how far you want to explore, or how many lives you wish to impact, you can excel and surpass many others by embracing the cherished passion that resides deep within your heart. This invaluable quality will serve as your guiding light on your life's journey. Therefore, when embarking on any endeavor, be sure to select what truly resonates with you.

Recognize that should the need to defend your choice arise, you can proudly stand by it, for nothing else will make as much sense. As you commence your journey, keep your eyes wide open and refrain from being blinded by external circumstances. Understand that disappointments may surface, and you may carry the weight of regret if you make hasty decisions.

Perhaps you are someone who has selected more than one path, unsure of what will ultimately unfold. You may find comfort in exploring various ideas and approaches that shape your identity. These may succeed or falter, but in order to attain lasting happiness and unwavering confidence in your pursuits, you must identify the guiding star within you. This is the element that will never let you down, unleashing your best self and illuminating your path with ease. You will find your true self, seamlessly integrating into whatever comes your way through this guiding star.

We often find ourselves drawn to what we love most, and sometimes, it aligns with our deepest desires, but disappointingly, it can let us down. There are moments when uncertainty looms over our chances of success, even though we eagerly invest ourselves in it, yielding little in return. Nevertheless, treasure the inner spark within you, as it refuses to settle for mediocrity. This is where your significance resides, where your deepest aspirations hold weight. For once in your life, you find belonging and inner peace.

Occasionally, instead of taking the easy path that appears deceptively simple, you might need to explore alternatives that coax out your best self. It's ironic how you can lose yourself to something temporarily purposeless, as you patiently wait for a change that never arrives.

Despite not realizing it, you possess a reservoir of patience within, though it often goes to waste on the wrong pursuits. Hidden within you lies the potential to inspire and amaze the world. This purpose has dwelled inside you for quite some time. How can you discern whether your current path aligns with your true self?

It's when you keep losing sight of your identity, disappearing further with every effort you invest, that you begin to wonder if you're on the right track. It's a peculiar experience, wishing for different outcomes and fearing that you might be running out of time to achieve your dreams.

Many times in life, we carry regrets that we can no longer change about ourselves. It's quite sad when a human life ends without achieving anything significant. You might have wished to be someone important, someone you believed you were meant to be, but it can be challenging to break through these barriers. Sometimes, it becomes so difficult that you don't know what to do anymore. However, you can keep pushing yourself to turn your dreams into reality, and eventually, you might make it happen.

However, achieving your dreams, whether it's becoming a star or attaining your goals, can sometimes haunt you. You may regret not reaching your aspirations earlier when everything felt crucial and mattered deeply to you. Fulfillment is often found by being exceptional when you're young, full of energy, and bursting with life. It may seem like it's taking longer than it should for things to happen.

Being early in pursuing your dreams might be your only chance to find happiness in yourself and what you've become. Don't let procrastination steal this opportunity. Time is precious, and you don't have to wait until it's too late. Strive to make your dreams a reality now, no matter what it takes. Be inspired by those who have faced similar challenges.

Remember, they are the ones who paved the way for people like us, providing a platform for those who aspire to achieve greatness. You might wonder what it means to be motivated and how external influences can shape your desires. Motivation often comes from observing qualities in others that resonate with your own aspirations. It's a reflection that you're not alone in your journey.

There is a lot out there that can inspire you, such as seeing someone's patience in pursuing their dreams and beliefs. Sometimes, you may feel like you've given your best effort and it's too late. But then, someone else comes along who has achieved the same thing, and their dedication motivates you to keep pushing.

Sometimes, you might feel like you've spent a lifetime working tirelessly to make something happen. Then, you see someone whose life has become a testament to holding onto their true passion. It might seem like madness to persist with unwavering determination, waiting patiently for success. But what matters most is that, eventually, it happens.

Talent can also be a great source of motivation. When you witness people who have dedicated their lives to their passions, it urges you to work even harder, even when achieving your goals seems challenging. Deep down, you know you can't ignore your true calling. You must let the world know who you are, even if it's not easy, and you may doubt yourself along the way.

So, you commit your life to this purpose, leaving behind your old self and shedding your past identity. Now, you've become someone with a voice, seeking an audience to listen. Despite the difficulties you've faced, you finally find your path.

This could be the kind of effort we need to possess. When you step out there, you may forget about what everyone is striving for and abandon the idea of needing an opportunity to make a living. Instead, envision yourself as a shining star, patiently waiting for the day when you'll finally have the chance to showcase your full potential and live confidently.

You will have to pick yourself up, recognizing that you have no other purpose except to be the person who overcame the most challenging situations. That's what life will throw at you – events that require you to focus less on your past and more on being the unique individual who found a way to achieve something exceptional in their life.

If you see yourself as a star who has fallen in love with everything the world has to offer, you'll understand that you must strive for success no matter the cost. People have various qualities in life, and you can learn a great deal by admiring individuals who excel in their work. So, venture out into the world and choose the path that aligns with your true aspirations. Your time will come when you inspire those who recognize your unique talents. Remember, finding motivation in others is fine, but it's our own work that sets us apart. We're not trying to copy someone else; we find strength in pursuing what we love most together.

How do you bring about peace while holding onto a secret without feeling the urge to share it with the world? Such a life would seem unfulfilled. We all have dreams and ambitions that have become an integral part of our existence.

These aspirations are vital to our humanity. We make numerous sacrifices for the things we love most. We dedicate our lives to achieving the visions we hold dear, often giving up a great deal to reach that level where our heartfelt desires can transform us. What does it mean to truly long for something to the point where you'd do anything to make it happen? How deeply does it resonate with you, and has it become the sole voice guiding your actions?

Love is when you release everything that doesn't align with your true desires and intentions. You shed the aspects of yourself that are not in harmony with your goals and remain steadfast in your pursuit. We are often influenced by external factors, like the stars we aspire to become, which can pull us in different directions. We find ourselves entangled in pursuits that do not align with our chosen path. To stay on the right course, we must let go of what does not define us and concentrate on what is meant for the journey we are on. External forces may attempt to pull us back to our starting point and cling to our former selves, but the yearning for all that lies ahead should allow us to shed the remnants of our past.

True love is a force that drives us towards creation. It doesn't matter what type of love we experience; its purpose is to break down barriers and awaken something profound within us. Deep within our hearts, there exists a burning desire for the world around us to come to life. At times, we grapple with the uncertainty of how to make our dreams a reality, and when our efforts seem fruitless, it can feel like a curse from the universe. This is when our yearning intensifies, and we dedicate ourselves to transforming our innermost passions into tangible realities.

No matter what form our love takes, whether it's a fascination with the stars or a quest for greatness, or even an attachment to certain aspects of life, we mustn't let them wither or vanish. Have faith in your uniqueness, and hold a steadfast belief in your ability to succeed. Why should you not achieve your dreams when you possess the roadmap to reach the stars and attain your deepest desires? Imagine a life burdened by unfulfilled goals; what name would you give yourself in a world where your aspirations slip through your fingers like sand?

Chapter Thirteen

Walk out of death

You've been stuck in this creative rut for a very long time, much longer than you expected. You haven't had the chance to focus on anything else that truly matters, and you've let many opportunities slip by. You're almost old enough to have a family of your own, but you haven't achieved those milestones. Your relentless pursuit of fame has chained you to your work every day. You might be wondering what you'd do if you failed, as you've been waiting for a meaningful idea that hasn't come yet.

The world of stardom has a strong grip on you, and you're constantly working day and night to reach recognition. Many forces are pushing against your efforts, and right now, you feel insignificant, waiting for that once-in-a-lifetime opportunity to arise. Your tireless efforts are preparing you for that day because you can't afford to fail; it's your only shot at being successful. You're not exactly failing, but there are numerous delays hindering your progress.

It's always been clear that perfection takes time, and now you're recovering from the uncertainty that came with feeling lost. You have a clearer sense of what you want and how to achieve it, even though the future can be unpredictable. Just because you're not making a substantial living from your passion yet doesn't mean you'll never reap any rewards from your involvement. It feels like you've dedicated yourself in vain, but that might not be the case in the end.

However, deep inside, you sense that in the distant future, not too far from where you are now, things will start to become clearer. It's time to adopt a positive outlook and release the insecurities and elements that don't align with your true self. While you encounter various situations and make new friends along the journey, it can sometimes feel quite solitary because not everyone can relate to your feelings.

You might find yourself compelled to let go of anything that no longer serves your interests or aligns with your vision. In your mind, you understand the importance of focusing solely on your goals and finding a partner who whole-heartedly shares their love and commitment. You desire an honorable companion who will bring joy and remain by your side forever.

Finding such a deep commitment can be challenging, especially when you're not entirely sure of your path. However, by releasing what doesn't resonate with your heart's desires and making room for your true self, you increase the chances of encountering a compatible partner and living happily ever after. This becomes possible as you forsake things that clearly do not belong in your life and create space for what truly defines you and fulfills your innermost desires.

Do you ever notice the things you bring into your life, the ones you hold onto, even though deep down, you know they won't be a part of your future self? Sometimes, we get stuck with stuff that doesn't align with our desires. But now that you feel a bit left behind, you realize you've accumulated a lot that doesn't serve any purpose.

But here's the real truth: You can never be too late for something you truly love, something that has found a place at the core of your heart. If only you could break through, there's so much that's worthy of you waiting ahead. All it takes is dedicating your life to it, and it could become a lifestyle that supports your happiness and success.

Don't be afraid to change, because when you chase your true passions, fame and fortune can bring fresh starts. It may have felt like you gave up on what truly mattered for a while, but the reality is you didn't. You just took a break to focus on what truly inspires your creative spirit.

Life has moments when you need to be content. It helps you stand tall and focus on what truly matters, like your responsibilities. Being responsible doesn't mean you can't strive for more. You have obligations, but a part of you yearns for a deeper purpose, like shining as a star. You don't want to settle for being an ordinary person; challenges inspire you.

You live with the eagerness to be recognized, even if you start small. You believe you can grow into everything you desire, and that speaks volumes about your true self. It doesn't matter how weak you feel right now; what matters is finding a place where your ideas belong. A place that provides a platform for your growth and helps you become stronger while expanding your vision.

We often rush to complete tasks early to ensure we don't get left behind. Until you get things right, many efforts seem meaningless, especially concerning what you truly want. Sometimes, unexpected situations can seriously delay your progress, almost as if they're intentional obstacles. Life tests us on various aspects of creation to see if we truly want to become who we are, even if it goes against the current.

When you've dedicated yourself to succeed, following the right path, and finally reach your destination, that's when you can truly be yourself on the platform you've chosen.

Why don't you consider the path you've been on? You've worked really hard, and everything you've done has been preparing you for this journey you're embarking on. Finding someone to love and commit to would mean a lot and mark a fresh start, a clean slate where you can be happy. Just remember not to spoil it by being dishonest. Good and meaningful relationships are hard to come by, and searching for them can be challenging. There are many obstacles you might encounter if you don't handle things properly.

A lot is clear, especially when you look back at how you got to this point in your life. Losing a true companion was a big part of it, and without that kind of person in your life, you might not have felt valuable. We all have temptations that can get in the way, and without discipline, you could easily get sidetracked and jeopardize what you stand for. True love is essential, and it can make the world feel more stable. Without a good partner, you might feel isolated, struggling to find a place where you're accepted and cared for.

You can't know everything; there are limits to what you can understand. But discipline can help you reach a high level of understanding. Remember, not doing things right or not behaving properly can weaken you. We can excel in parts of our lives where we organize ourselves well. That's how you can put the knowledge you've gained to good use when the opportunity arises. Now is the time to demonstrate what you've learned and stay focused on your goal, as it will capture the interest of many and set you apart.

By consistently focusing on what you know, you can avoid failure. There may have been times when failure seemed likely, but the knowledge you've acquired through your dedication to creativity can unleash something extraordinary deep within you. You can overcome challenging situations and setbacks, even when hope appears lost, and find meaning in things that may have seemed meaningless.

What we do in life can either enhance or diminish our value, and this can happen when you lose hope in your creative pursuits. When you become disconnected from the evolving world, despite your efforts to reinvent yourself, it's crucial to stay disciplined and connected to reality. This will bring you closer to understanding what the modern world demands from you. Properly comprehending and conducting yourself is the key to unlocking your true human potential. It allows you to tap into your innate intelligence, deep within, and mold your life in a more positive direction.

Regardless of what led you to embark on your unique journey, it's common for people to lose interest in old habits or their former selves. Initially, the idea of change and transformation might have seemed straightforward, but finding lasting meaning and happiness often requires significant effort and doing things right. Achieving self-contentment can be challenging, especially when you're navigating a different path from your past. You may have felt unworthy of your current self, but remember that our experiences shape us into who we are. Obtaining what you desire and finding satisfaction may require more effort than you initially anticipated.

While it might seem difficult, you can definitely find your unique path in life and discover what truly brings you success and fulfillment. Sometimes, we may lose our way in becoming the best version of ourselves until we learn to understand something special that leads us to contentment. It's okay to hold onto who you used to be, but there are moments when letting go of the past becomes the better option, especially when it no longer serves you well.

Releasing your past, when it no longer serves a meaningful purpose, can be a good decision. You can't keep clinging to things that no longer benefit you. There is a chance that you can uncover something extraordinary, and sometimes, you just need to trust that the path you're on is guided by righteousness and a desire for greatness. If you're willing to leave yesterday behind, your best life might be waiting for you around the corner, where your happiness remains uncompromised, and you're free to be yourself.

Don't miss out on the opportunity to explore this world because you're afraid to try something new. Embracing your talents grants you unlimited potential and the power of free will, allowing you to pursue your deepest desires. It should feel natural to follow your passions, even if you don't know where the journey will lead. Who knows, it might just be the beginning of one of the greatest adventures known to humankind.

There's a hidden part of your life, waiting to be uncovered. It holds the power to unlock the energy within you and elevate you to a level where you shine as a unique beacon of understanding and creativity. As we stand here, it's clear that none of us are the absolute best, and sometimes, we tend to underestimate ourselves to the point where progress seems unattainable. So, what's the solution? You could either turn a blind eye to your current self and affirm that you'll achieve greatness.

Even if you resist, you might still face similar challenges in your current state. Standing where you are as the person you've become, you might struggle to reach success and happiness. Regardless, somewhere along life's journey, you must maintain enthusiasm for being a human being, believing deep within that you're destined for more. Continue to strive for what you truly love.

We all aspire to be recognized for our exceptional discoveries or unique accomplishments. But do we possess the courage to pursue those dreams? Often, you'll find yourself questioning whether you possess that rare gift that sets you apart from ordinary individuals. It's not merely about talent or being a star, as these attributes aren't innate to everyone. It's about the motivation and attitude we cultivate toward our deepest desires. When you dedicate yourself wholeheartedly to something you truly yearn for, that's when you truly stand out.

At some points in life, you may feel like you've given a lot. In those moments, it's essential to reflect on whether your efforts are sufficient for achieving true greatness. Should you devote your entire life to one pursuit, leaving behind your previous self? Is the approach of giving your all to what you love, without looking back, the key? Perhaps the attitude we bring to our desires holds the answer.

Consider if you haven't fully committed to your goal, lacking experience in what it truly demands. Maybe this is your first encounter with such a challenging task, drawing deeply from within you. What do you do when you can't imagine being without it? Do you invest your entire self and rely on luck to reach your goals, or do you work diligently, understanding your path?

You might not possess exceptional talent or a unique gift. So, how do you respond when your efforts don't yield success? Do you run away, feeling bewildered, or do you persist with determination and comprehension?

Ultimately, our deepest desire is to be loved and understood as human beings. We yearn to share our lives with the world, to be recognized for our abilities, and to find a place in people's hearts. We aim to be there for those isolated and abandoned by their loved ones, offering hope when it seems scarce. Perhaps possessing the power to motivate, encourage, and guide people back to reality is what we truly need.

Being a human being is a profound aspect of existence, woven into the very fabric of life, brimming with hope for those who depend on you. Understanding the struggles that many face, your role is to provide them with the strength to confront their fears. This understanding isn't something you can pretend; you've traversed your own hardships and encountered your own adversaries, enabling you to empathize with the challenges that all human beings encounter.

To truly prepare for this role, you must have personally weathered similar difficulties and setbacks, emerging victorious from such circumstances. It's not merely advice you offer, but a quality you transmit to every individual you encounter. This gift is one you generously share with all who know you, becoming a source of blessings and transformation in countless lives.

Reflecting on the life you lead, its meaning, and its origins, it becomes evident that this path requires a deep commitment to understanding and pursuing what you truly love, consistently achieving success through it. Although this isn't a journey one can undertake effortlessly on a daily basis, it is a deliberate life choice for those who are passionately committed to their aspirations.

Perhaps your current circumstances feel insufficient, leaving you undervalued and yearning for greater challenges. Yet, you recognize that within you lies a unique gift and an explosive spirit. This gift isn't limited to transforming the lives of others; it also promises to profoundly impact your own existence.

You believe you're something unique, unlike anything the world has ever seen. You don't underestimate humanity. You have a deep understanding of yourself, which serves as your motivation to achieve even more. You could have easily accepted failure, but your daily learning journey has enabled you to overcome potential obstacles. Now, the world is beckoning for your presence. Regardless of your current location, you're inspired to answer this call. We all start somewhere, and you refuse to settle for a life of mediocrity. You're determined to make progress.

You might have remained stuck longer than anticipated, finding a certain comfort in your situation. However, the time has come to elevate your understanding and confront more formidable challenges. While you can take pride in your past accomplishments, it's important to remember that the world is your next arena, challenging your comprehension.

Now, it's time to prepare yourself for what lies ahead. You are faced with the entirety of creation, and there's a great need for you to step out and inspire hope and faith in those who aspire to understand themselves better and grow. Many individuals are yearning to ascend to a higher level of understanding, seeking the strength to conquer whatever obstacles stand in their way. We are all human beings in search of purpose, and without it, life loses its significance.

Deep inside each of us, there exists a burning desire to make sacrifices in the present, all in the hopes that somewhere out there, the world eagerly anticipates the essence of who you are becoming. In the midst of life's intricate challenges, during those moments when we feel utterly lost, we discover an extraordinary power to triumph over adversity and grow stronger for it. You may have found yourself trapped in that deep abyss for longer than you ever imagined, but remember, the world doesn't halt there. It's merely the prologue to your true self, a chance to showcase your boundless potential.

It was through this unique journey that you came to realize that while it wasn't a walk in the park, there's nothing else you could have been. Your significance extends not only to yourself but also to every facet of our lives and the person you've evolved into as your ultimate aspiration. What might have initially seemed perplexing gradually evolved into the very essence of being human. Often, you may ponder where you could have been throughout your existence, neglecting yourself as you did, yet achieving your goals can restore your sense of pride and the values you uphold.

We all harbor countless desires that we aspire to fulfill, and perhaps it's the pursuit of true contentment that you genuinely seek. Until you reach that juncture in your life, you may feel somewhat adrift in what truly matters. As we wholeheartedly dedicate ourselves to what appears promising, which might involve striving for our dreams, sometimes we find that nothing truly justifies the immense effort we invest. You might even regret the path you've traversed to reach this point. It's as if we never needed to add anything to our current selves, and now everything appears to be malfunctioning, leaving you perplexed about how to mend this aspect of your entire being.

Is it possible to return to your former self, considering that so much of it existed from the very beginning? Although many things may not seem deserving of our attention, we can thrive through sheer determination. This willpower should remain close to your heart as a tool for success because you can no longer reverse the transformation you've undergone. Life was once beautiful before you encountered a multitude of challenges that made everything seem insurmountable.

However, if you are willing to put in the effort needed to achieve success, you can find happiness at the end of your journey. This path leads to a central point where all our endeavors are focused on bringing out the best in our creations. Despite the challenges that may arise, only through art and believing in your own potential can you navigate towards your desired destination. How did things spiral out of control so badly that only embracing your inner artist can help you recover from the turmoil that comes with feeling lost?

Don't let yourself down by persisting in a life that no longer brings you joy, while pondering the true essence of existence. Remember, it's all about embracing your uniqueness and not losing sight of it. Neglecting this aspect will leave you feeling adrift, constantly searching for your true identity, wondering what it truly signifies. It's when you possess a deep understanding of yourself that you become less influenced by external factors and people, allowing you to inhabit your own world.

The moment you learn to trust yourself is when you can start becoming self-reliant and experience true freedom. Relying on others to align with your own desires can often complicate even the simplest situations, making resolution elusive and leaving you feeling powerless. This does not contribute to our strength as individuals. We must acknowledge that together, as a collective, we shape our world, and there will be times when you can lean on others for support. However, there will also be moments when you realize that you must rely on yourself.

You can only rely on yourself because you can't predict when someone might let you down or simply move on. Commitment varies between people, and we all have different thoughts, which can make someone unreliable to trust with your whole life. To avoid future regrets, believe in yourself and prepare thoroughly for what you truly desire. This might be the only way to have a reliable foundation. When things go wrong, you'll have yourself to depend on, even when the truth isn't as trustworthy as your own understanding.

As you walk the path of creating your life, you become your own support. To have faith in your knowledge, you need to work hard until you're confident in your abilities. Regardless of how tough situations may get, trust in your intellectual capacity to find the right solutions that will positively impact your life. In a world filled with uncertainty, even the truth can become complicated, so you must clarify what you mean by "right."

Furthermore, remember that for something to be true, it must first exist within you. It's the spark planted like a seed in your soul, and as it grows, it shapes the reality you see in the outside world. This inner truth continues to expand until it fills your entire being, guiding you along your path with purpose.

What makes you unique is that you've chosen a path in life, and you're committed to it. You know that no matter how vast life is, you'll stick to this path. It's the foundation of your faith, and you're confident that your interest in it won't lead to disappointment. This is what can help you escape the difficult situation you're in, and it won't let you down.

Even though our bodies may weaken, our faith becomes a powerful force within us that can't be shaken. It's what you trust wholeheartedly. There might come a time when your old ways of thinking and the knowledge you hold are overpowered by reality, and everything changes suddenly. You might try to adapt, but things can keep getting worse.

In the end, you may feel like a lifeless body, a weary person who couldn't reach their heart's desires. You might even feel like you've spiritually died before finding true love and settling into a marriage. You were preparing for so much, and then, in an instant, it all seems to fade away. It's as if you never became anything.

In that moment, you realize that not living is worse than physical death. It's like disappearing spiritually, and your deepest desires remain unfulfilled. But now, you're left with something you've identified as your source of strength and understanding. It's what gives you hope to overcome any situation or setback and become victorious once more.

Time has the power to challenge many aspects of our lives. When you've chosen a path, the duration it takes to reach your goals can be both a burden and an opportunity for growth. The length of a project can test your resilience before you're ready to conquer the world with your knowledge, and it might even overwhelm you at times. When you truly understand yourself and your purpose, you gain insight into what may have held you back in the past, and you can prepare for the future.

The present is a precious gift, shaped by our past efforts. From birth, we're equipped with the tools to navigate daily life. It's our unique human nature that leads to constant evolution, sometimes deviating from our original selves. But if you manage to overcome these challenges, you'll find true freedom. You'll reach a point where everything you hold dear is in harmony, guiding you back to your authentic self.

To reach this place, hard work and a thirst for knowledge are essential. Nurturing your passions and desires with love is the key. In the end, practicing love and understanding can lead to happiness and fulfillment. While the journey may be challenging, especially when everything aligns to support your daily life, it's worth the effort.

We are born into a regular world, surrounded by all the things that creation has made for us to enjoy. But when you start wanting to be different, it's almost like awakening a certain spirit that thrives on limiting a person's potential. It seems like we can't fully be ourselves without having to sacrifice some part of who we truly are. When you become tired of the way we live our lives and begin exploring other possibilities for finding fulfillment in this vast world, it's as if you're starting to resent yourself.

Doing the same thing over and over isn't the path to being truly human. When you no longer find satisfaction in what used to make you happy, you can rediscover yourself with love in a universe that will never reject your true identity. It's our own unique creation within this vast and immense reality that can bring us closer to our desires and make us feel more alive.

Sometimes, it's said that "birth is like death," and perhaps we've been misled when we believed we were pushing ourselves toward a better life. Somewhere deep within, a part of us dies because we can never return to the old normal and live exactly as we once did, following our true dreams. Each of us is unique and contributes to the grand scheme of things, not only for ourselves but also for others. To realize this and give a piece of yourself back to people, you must push your entire being to its utmost potential.

This forms the basis of genuine love, which we extend to all our commitments. It plays a significant role in shaping the future experiences we will encounter in our lives. To truly build the life we desire, we must first dedicate ourselves wholeheartedly. It is our responsibility to give everything we have to our aspirations, even when pursuing our true desires might challenge our core values and involve complex decisions.

Through our own understanding and knowledge, we are capable of connecting with a world designed for us to comprehend. This enables us to begin experiencing the love we hold for the things we desire. We discover satisfaction in many of our endeavors, as much of what we achieve is not accidental but the result of our determination to attain greatness. We become more aware of the events occurring around us, opening our hearts and making an enduring commitment to what lies deep within us.

This necessity arises from our true selves; we must embrace this concept initially, as it forms the foundation upon which all subsequent actions are built, fueled by our genuine self-love. This extends to the relationships we forge with those who will accompany us throughout our entire lives. In the past, perhaps, we may have been tempted to pretend that our love was true when we knew deep down that it was not.

Now, we can no longer deceive ourselves. We must offer a love that resonates with our essence, a love that is genuinely felt and cannot be misunderstood. Our current connection to the world and all that exists is authentic, a sincere longing to unite with our innermost selves or even potentially heal our place within this expansive creation. People are born into this world uncertain whether they emerged from true love or mere desire, often left wondering why everything they touch seems to shatter, and their reception falls short of their expectations by all living beings.

Perhaps many things could have been improved if you wholeheartedly dedicated yourself to them. Now, it's not possible to change who you are, and you can't promise full commitment to someone else. If you haven't planted the seed of true love deep in your heart, no one can commit to you, no matter how much you ask.

It's crucial to understand the significance of such love and dedication in shaping your identity. You must fully commit to your chosen path, making it your top priority. When we invest so much of ourselves, we experience profound emotions. You may have wondered how to achieve your goals, but true love resides within us, waiting to be channeled in the direction of our aspirations.

Now, you aspire to genuine commitment and a love like never before. You deserve the best because, at times, we haven't received what we truly deserve in past commitments, even before our birth. From the very essence of your being, you can conclude that the love that has shaped you is authentic.

However, at this moment, a golden opportunity has presented itself, allowing us to extract the utmost joy and fulfillment from our existence. It's the chance to experience a profound, authentic love that you may not have even realized existed. This love won't solely be confined to your romantic relationships; rather, it will encompass all your deepest desires in this current chapter of life. Moreover, it possesses the power to mend the wounds inflicted by the misfortunes we've endured due to a deficiency in this precious heritage of love.

This phenomenon is an undeniable aspect of our identity. You could traverse the globe in search of it, only to discover that it resides within you. To attain it, you must exert relentless effort, dedicating it first to your heart's truest desires with unwavering commitment. Ensure its authenticity, for this sincerity will dictate the quality of care and devotion you receive in return, ultimately cultivating the happiness we, as human beings, so desperately seek.

This love will magnetize everything genuine within your being, imbuing your life with its perpetual presence. It will only find its true place when your commitment saturates your entire essence. Perhaps you once believed that what you possessed was all there was to it, but it's only when it transforms into a love worthy of your true self that it seamlessly integrates into every facet of your existence.

Chapter Fourteen

Taste of success

It's about what we've dedicated our lives to, and we should remember that the efforts we put into what we love the most can bring us something in return. Sometimes, we forget what we've committed ourselves to because we're involved in so many things. However, there might be that one thing for which you've sacrificed everything to see it happen. You could be someone who has made many attempts, and as human beings, we often try different things. Some of our efforts bear fruit, while we give up on others.

If you never decide what you want to live for, you may not realize what you've truly committed yourself to, and this can hinder your understanding of your purpose. You might have acquired a lot of knowledge, but there will be one thing that defines your life. This is how you'll face the world when you no longer have the time to explore new interests. This is when you'll understand the importance of dedicating yourself to something deserving of your attention, and you won't even remember what you used to be.

The truth is, we won't always have the chance to do everything that pleases us. We often engage in various activities without realizing that one day, we'll have to leave them all behind. Hobbies and interests will no longer matter; it will be about what you've become skilled at. You may start something as a hobby, but it could end up being the sole purpose of your life. If you're truly devoted and believe in a particular idea, it can become your path to freedom from anything that tries to hold you captive or imprison you.

So much in life can be uncertain, as we grapple with the complexities of the world we inhabit. Our knowledge is limited to understanding ourselves, and we hope that our perceptions align with some aspect of reality. While we stand firm in our beliefs, we can never fully predict the actions of others, leaving us with only our own judgment to rely upon. Therefore, it is crucial to make thoughtful decisions regarding our aspirations. Recognizing when we have invested enough in a particular endeavor allows us to discern what truly defines us and shapes our lifelong journey.

Despite the vast array of opportunities and destinies before us, once we discover our true desires, we can establish a connection that reflects our essence. Through discipline and dedication, we can gain a profound understanding of this connection. This enduring bond safeguards us from disappointments and serves as a defense against our own potential pitfalls. The world's perception of us is intricately linked to our self-image, and it can either pave the way to success or obstruct our path. We must acknowledge that we can never be everything to everyone; we are human beings, driven by our heart's desires. When we wholeheartedly commit to a purpose, it has the power to breathe life into our aspirations.

In this world that often seeks to engulf us, it is essential to retain our sense of purpose and carry out our actions with integrity. Ultimately, our failures and setbacks do not define us, for true humanity finds its source of happiness irrespective of such challenges. Embracing the mindset of "whatever it takes" can be the foundation of our faith, potentially leading us to a place where life becomes more manageable.

What you will discover is that you have the unique ability to liberate yourself, as it has always been evident that a significant portion of your life relies on your actions to reach your goals. We all have our differences, and our aspirations vary from person to person. This is something we must learn to embrace about one another. When you pursue your passions wholeheartedly, it should be sufficient to fulfill your desires and bring inner peace. Achieving what you truly want with unwavering dedication should provide complete satisfaction, regardless of others' opinions about your creative endeavors.

However, when you become aware of the challenges the world presents, it can leave you feeling vulnerable and frustrated. Many obstacles may obstruct our path to what we cherish most. Yet, mastering a skill and excelling in it can set us free. So, before you consider the vast universe as a hindrance to your deepest desires, ask yourself if you possess the key to unlock the doors leading to your innermost dreams and happiness.

Have you found the strength within you to embrace your true self, or do you still feel pursued by inner demons from your past? What is it that troubles our spirits and refuses to let go of our former selves? Could it be that we come from difficult or challenging backgrounds, and our pasts continue to haunt us? Nevertheless, if you persist in leading yourself forward without dwelling on your past, you can break free from its grasp and forge a new path for yourself.

If only you had dedicated yourself to a noble cause that truly captured your attention, you might not find yourself entangled in an intractable predicament today. Often, we invest our time and energy in various pursuits, but do these endeavors align with our inner selves? Can the object of your faith rescue you from this seemingly insurmountable situation? Perhaps you never fully prepared for the challenges of the outside world. Somehow, you anticipated an easy journey, assuming you could effortlessly achieve your aspirations. However, you failed to comprehend that our actions shape our destinies.

As you grapple with the difficulties of moving forward, you gradually recognize that reality doesn't always match our initial perceptions. The path you once envisioned as friendly and straightforward has proven to be more daunting than expected, leaving you feeling trapped. In your current state of self-reflection, you contemplate the purpose of your existence. If only you had thoroughly equipped yourself for the myriad experiences awaiting you in the world beyond, you might not feel permanently ensnared. There comes a pivotal moment when one stands at a crossroads, compelled to make a choice. To navigate this juncture effectively, you must have diligently cultivated a moral compass to guide your decisions.

Irrespective of whether your journey has been arduous or relatively smooth, you must possess the resilience to interpret the lessons encountered along the way. Life embodies both pain and love, and no experience is beyond the realm of meaningful interpretation. Through an artistic perspective, we summon the fortitude to tackle our problems and confront the adversities that cross our path. However, we must be vigilant, for allowing these challenges to dictate our lives could imperil the very values we hold dear, including the love we share with one another.

Being decisive is essential for finding your path in life. You can't remain stuck in something you want to pursue throughout your life. Sometimes, you may feel trapped in your soul, wishing for a better way, and refusing to accept defeat due to your current circumstances. You strive to reach for something that truly reflects your worth, enduring the pain and longing to dedicate yourself wholly to what truly matters. When you had more time, you didn't realize the world was waiting for you, and love was calling. However, you couldn't answer that call because you still needed to complete your journey, which would determine how far you could go.

How could you have known that you would fall in love with creation and embark on this journey while you were still young? It gave you the chance to follow a path that wouldn't disappoint you. Dedicate yourself to something that will always be your source of strength, courage, and genuine love, something that will never let you down throughout your life. This way, you can weather the ups and downs, and when it's time to love and take on responsibilities, you'll be well-prepared to offer a deep commitment to someone deserving.

True fulfillment comes from dedicating yourself to something while you still have the chance, and it eventually becomes your legacy. Once you find that thing, give it your all because you know it will reward you in proportion to your dedication. You might wonder where you've been on your journey, asking questions about the passage of time and where you should be. However, you'll realize that you've been maturing, understanding that not everything we devote our lives to aligns with our age.

Choosing to commit to something later in life can prevent you from reaching your full potential. This is because the most incredible feeling is discovering yourself at the right moment and arriving exactly where you need to be. This journey can reveal the incredible and boundless potential that resides within us. The entire world then becomes your playground, the place of your birth, and with so many demands around us, you become the perfect fit for the situation.

In our early stages, we often fail to see the larger picture. Much has been designed to make life more challenging for human beings, and we tend to focus solely on our current selves, thinking that we can make things work once we reach a certain point in life. However, as time goes on, we start to comprehend the need to fight hard for things to make sense. Despite clinging to our ideas, nothing seems to align with the greater context of humanity. If we make a mistake at this point, we must start from scratch and undo all that we have done.

Where can we find the world aligning precisely with our predictions? Where have we made the right choices, and everything we understand about creation holds true? It's important to choose something from the beginning that you know will never waste your time. Unlike many people who cling to things that no longer serve a purpose, you must let go of them and embark on a journey that will define your identity.

Perhaps we have been holding onto our youth, and the things we cling to refuse to grow with us. While we remain young at heart on the inside, the world is rapidly changing around us, and time continues to pass.

No matter what you do, it's important not to stray too far from the truth. This way, when the need for change arises, you'll be able to address any issues that come up. It's better to avoid getting lost in confusion because you didn't think things through carefully. Instead of finding yourself stuck and unable to repair the damage, you should hold onto that inner desire to become so much more.

You have a strong desire to progress to a higher level of understanding because you know you deserve a chance to improve your current situation. To make this possible, you need to know how to simplify your life by focusing only on what truly matters.

Along the way, it's important to commit wholeheartedly to something, understanding that you can't be something else. To make this commitment meaningful, it should be a decision you've carefully considered, and you should proceed with caution as you navigate through life's challenges.

We can't predict the future with absolute certainty; our view is limited by our own horizons. Therefore, it's crucial to make wise choices to avoid future regrets. It's unfortunate to think that with equal opportunities, you could have enjoyed a better quality of life. However, if you allow certain mistakes to persist in your daily life, you'll have to live with the consequences, compromising your well-being.

When you reach a point where you can no longer exercise your free will, you may miss the opportunity to become whatever you truly desire in this world. Failing to extract genuine value from various aspects of life, such as relationships, may allow us to deceive others in certain areas, but it's unlikely that we will find true love. As you navigate the journey of life's creation, it's crucial to be cautious about the decisions you make, regardless of your inherent abilities. There are aspects of life where you know you can reach your utmost potential, and this is when your unique talents become a reliable foundation.

As you progress along the path of understanding, there are certain things you can come to terms with, while others may remain elusive, like the quest for love. Deep down, you may possess a reservoir of untapped potential, and you trust yourself to accomplish something extraordinary. However, to truly excel in this endeavor, you must exhibit unwavering determination and dedication, never looking back. If you still have alternative options in a world where you aim to make a significant impact, you're not truly succeeding.

When you commit yourself wholeheartedly to a noble cause, remember that neglecting seriousness in certain aspects of life can have dire consequences, potentially shattering a human existence irreparably. Live with a profound understanding of what this means, carrying your purpose in your heart. Lead a fulfilling life, marked by accomplishments from start to finish, even if not every step of the way. Find contentment in the journey.

When you feel like time is slipping away from you, it's crucial to pursue success relentlessly, no matter the challenges you face. Don't allow external circumstances to dominate your thoughts because they don't belong there. Instead, let your heart be filled with genuine love, not just for individuals but for everything, including yourself. This love should encompass all aspects of life, emphasizing the importance of quality in everything you do. It should strive to create positivity in your surroundings without allowing time to pass in vain. Such love defines your identity and understanding, as mere knowledge alone doesn't suffice.

Avoid becoming your own obstacle, even when you possess the knowledge and skills to rectify situations gone awry. Never judge yourself as unworthy or undeserving, resigning to a life of mediocrity, despite knowing that you are capable of achieving so much more. Success varies from person to person, but in the end, it all boils down to the same desire – to excel in your chosen path and validate your worthiness. You want to demonstrate to yourself that your aspirations are grounded in reality, not mere fantasies. Regardless of the unique definition of success for each individual, understanding your true self and believing in your abilities is paramount.

Nonetheless, you require a vital key to unlock the doors to success in your life. Even if you've made significant progress and believe you deserve the best life has to offer, unforeseen challenges can erode your confidence, reminding you of the uncertainties of existence. In such moments of self-reflection, ask yourself what may have shaken your confidence or led you to doubt your capabilities, despite all the knowledge and potential you possess.

Feeling like you're denied your true self or what you rightly deserve can leave you with a heavy burden. Even if you don't possess exceptional talents, you believe that life should have some purpose, and you know you have a sharp mind. You also care about the world around you. You've been marked by the unknown, and it's challenging to find your way out of that dark place or prepare for a life filled with setbacks.

Could it be that at some point in our lives, we must commit ourselves to something, even if it means facing death? Death might seem preferable to a life without meaning. Maybe we focus on too many things and lose ourselves, unable to repair the damage caused by our lack of complete commitment to our desires.

Success in your endeavors can unleash something within you, although it's hard to believe in this when you're stuck at the beginning. It's difficult to imagine seeing your true passion come to life for the first time. This is what we strive for—to see our own will become reality. When you resist conforming to the world's ways and believe in your unique approach, you gain a profound understanding of the world around you.

Your ideas hold great significance. Having a distinctive perspective on life doesn't mean you want everyone to conform to it. You simply have a special concept that resides within you, shaping the values you hold dear. Now, it yearns to manifest in the world outside, not out of selfishness but because dreams must be fulfilled and transformed into success. We live for many things, but the uncompromisable value lies in staying true to your essence.

Whether we're young or old, we all have something we love deeply, something we can't live without seeing become real. But the world can be tough when we have such dreams because not everyone understands them. So many people find comfort in the ordinary, and they might not support our creative ambitions. Following our dreams can be hard on our well-being, and we can lose unnecessary things along the way. It can feel overwhelming as we go through this journey of growth.

However, as we pursue our deepest desires, our inner selves transform into what we long to be. Despite the challenges we faced, the pain fades, and our focus shifts to achieving success. We overcome obstacles until we embody the spirit that brings our desires to life. We become more than our physical selves, learning to manifest our needs. We aim for the star born from our longing, turning our dreams into reality.

This journey isn't an everyday occurrence. We may give our all to make our dreams come true, and sometimes, it doesn't happen as quickly as we'd like. We might feel stuck in a spiritual limbo as our desires resist becoming reality. Only after we've done everything correctly do we start to thrive. It's crucial to develop ourselves according to our true potential, honing our skills, and eventually, we attain what once seemed unattainable, shaping our lives in the process.

When you have experienced and overcome numerous challenges, you can take pride in your unwavering determination to turn your dreams into reality. Reflect on the journey of self-improvement you embarked upon until your ideas evolved into manageable endeavors. Imagine the sensation of forging ahead despite your initial uncertainty, driven by an innate desire to transform possibilities into actualities. Even when you found yourself adrift in the labyrinth of life, you steadfastly resisted succumbing to self-doubt, nurturing the conviction that you possessed the capability to correct course, no matter how many stumbles along the way. Who could have predicted such wisdom from the outset?

We conceive ideas, nurture them, and nurture the belief that they will thrive, even when the path forward appears elusive. We toil until we begin to discern the path we've carved out. In a world teeming with diverse, exceptional, and singular thoughts, we contribute our own, firmly convinced that it holds a place in the grand tapestry of creation. We do not simply envision it as another invention; we brim with the confidence of its ultimate success. This is not to diminish the merits of others' endeavors; rather, it is a recognition of the formidable challenges that abound in our complex universe. Nevertheless, our minds remain steadfastly anchored in the pursuit of success.

We commit ourselves wholeheartedly, shunning opportunism, and confront life in all its enigmatic uncertainty with unwavering patience. We navigate through a myriad of trials, steadfast in the belief that knowledge and patience will ultimately lead us to our destination. If countless others have achieved their aspirations, so can we. What sets us apart? Are we not deserving of the person we aspire to be? Who can gauge the measure of our worthiness and what we truly merit

At first, many things could have gone wrong, but you didn't let those setbacks determine the course of your life indefinitely. Instead, you developed strength by embracing qualities like determination. You needed to constantly remind yourself that you knew what you were doing, even when faced with numerous challenges that made you feel inadequate. However, you remained loyal to your goals.

Loyalty is truly tested when you encounter adversities, and success is influenced by a multitude of factors, often accompanied by the fear of failure. At times, it may seem as though being human comes with constant denial. This struggle can persist for a significant duration, depending on your level of commitment and your approach.

The journey through these trials of commitment isn't simple unless you are fully dedicated to your aspirations. If the pursuit of success truly ignites your inner drive, you can elevate your life to a level you never thought possible. It's crucial to remember that you aim to make your mark in this vast universe. Therefore, you must maintain unwavering discipline and put forth your best efforts until you achieve your desired outcome.

The nature of success is a topic of contemplation: does the method used to achieve it matter, or is the outcome and your happiness the only significant aspects? Perhaps, after discovering your unique approach, adapting as necessary, and making life changes, you now feel entitled to enjoy whatever life has to offer. Does the path to success hold significance, or is it the ultimate achievement and your personal happiness that truly matter? Throughout this journey, you held onto a vision, knowing it had never existed before, and you made it a reality for the first time.

Creating a lasting legacy isn't something you inherit; instead, you become the originator of a unique concept that becomes an integral part of reality, particularly for those who come after your time has passed. Your goal is to establish a thriving legacy that paves the way for everyone in your life. So, in the end, have we all succeeded, or is it me who has achieved success because I persevered with those ideas until they became clear? You may grapple with certain ideas and fail, but I managed to transform them into a tangible, comprehensible reality.

Although not everything in our journey fills us with pride, some of the challenges we encounter are situations we could have navigated more effectively if we weren't burdened by responsibilities. However, given the obligations that come with everything we undertake, we must stay focused on our pursuits, which can sometimes feel like a prolonged journey. Opportunities may arise, but we must often disregard them, focusing only on what directly relates to our current endeavors. It's especially satisfying when these align perfectly with the principles we've established as our guiding rules from the outset.

Even when faced with a multitude of ideas put forth by various individuals, our preparedness to make the right choices remains crucial. This is why we must distance ourselves from the noise, as others may create things that hold no significance for us. It's essential to avoid becoming entangled in something that doesn't reflect your true self, especially if it holds no personal importance. Understanding the rationale behind waiting for your true purpose to manifest is key.

Imagine your world and how vast it can be. Visualize the boundaries that encapsulate everything you are and everything you can be. This perspective is key to comprehending your aspirations and the steps needed to accomplish them.

Before you can distinguish yourself and truly shine, you must strive for excellence. This is where you not only meet expectations but go beyond, reaping additional rewards. There's a wealth of wisdom to gain from those who have poured their heart and soul into their pursuits, creating something worthy of study.

Perhaps, from another viewpoint, you can pay it forward, sharing your unique insights with others. Despite our similarities, each of us walks a different path, shaped by our distinct experiences. Have you observed the world through your own eyes? What motivated you to rise up and share your voice? It's because you've glimpsed your own universe, a one-of-a-kind reality that makes our lives special, and this becomes the life we share with others.

Live to see the inner passions and dreams you hold dear manifest in the world. When you encounter beauty, strive to incorporate that beauty into every facet of your being for all to admire. It may even become your livelihood. Regardless of your starting point or how long it took to understand, reveal your true self, as we yearn to witness your thoughts materialize in the physical realm. Are you sometimes hesitant to express your innermost thoughts? Perhaps that's precisely what you've been doing, but you just haven't found the right way to externalize them.

Intelligence can sometimes shape how you express your inner thoughts and dreams. You may have a clear idea, but the way you perceive things may not align with the world around you. Your viewpoint, the platform you stand on, and your level of thinking can influence your reality, but remember that your version of reality may not be universal. Perhaps we create things to connect with a specific audience or set limits on how far we're willing to go. Do you see yourself achieving your goals on a global scale, and are you willing to make the necessary efforts?

Success becomes the reward for your actions, whether you make a global impact or find fulfillment in your current circumstances. It's through your actions that you discover who you truly are. The world is full of diverse minds and perspectives, which can sometimes challenge your intelligence. You can't predict how others think, but whether you pursue your goals in the way you've envisioned or live a more conventional life, both paths can lead to personal growth.

Your journey, your experiences, your moments of feeling lost, and the sacrifices you've made all contribute to reaching a point where you find true satisfaction within yourself. It's not just about achieving temporary goals; it's about becoming the person you were meant to be.

Chapter Fifteen

Everyone wanted that

You may not know why you started seeing life this way, but one thing is certain: we all have the potential to make a positive impact on the world. Whether you're inspired by someone else or you have a deep inner belief that you can achieve something remarkable, it shapes the way we lead our lives. Along the journey, there must be someone who takes the initiative and becomes a trailblazer.

It's a wonderful feeling to be the person who brings forth a unique idea that others have struggled to reach. However, creating a new concept and succeeding with it is not an easy task. Sometimes, groundbreaking ideas have to start somewhere, and it's astonishing what people can come up with. Knowing that your vision is not merely influenced by someone else's thoughts but stems from your own inner conviction that you can change life as we know it.

We often never anticipate such accomplishments from ourselves, often regarding those who have invented remarkable things as extraordinary individuals. You might not have expected to become a part of that category, but it's a part of personal growth to be inspired by someone's creative work. Whether you're drawn to the innovative thinking of a young or experienced person, you can't always be certain about how people become who they are. What you do know is how you arrived where you are today.

Your journey involved overcoming numerous challenges and choosing a path different from the mainstream. Deep down, it's not about being ignorant; instead, it's about recognizing the significant role you play in the creative process. While you may desire to lead a life that conforms to everyone's expectations, your daily existence is also characterized by this novel perspective that resides solely in your mind. It might be challenging for many to relate to, but it's an integral part of your unique journey.

How can we become something unique, something that only exists within ourselves? How do we recognize a need in the world that many are unaware of? Even before it becomes a reality, how can we sense that it will have a significant impact? Perhaps we could have followed the path of conformity, living our lives as mere followers of others, or maybe we could have lived without purpose.

However, your heart possesses the ability to discern the profound needs that people have to find happiness within themselves. You may ponder countless questions, such as how you transformed into the person you are today. You've become a resilient individual determined to bring about greatness in your surroundings. The world may attempt to influence you through exposure to a global community, but if you genuinely care, everything will fall into place. You carry the purity of heart that allows you to see possibilities where others see none, and through this, you can create opportunities even in seemingly impossible situations.

We all have our unique perspectives on the world and our surroundings. Yet, having the ability to identify significant concerns is a rare gift. It's not something that many possess, and it's shaped by the kind of person you are, your interpretations of your experiences, and the wisdom you've gained.

While we may observe and understand the same things, some lack the capacity to give to others. No one is inherently endowed with the virtue to be what others cannot be. This distinction is largely determined by how you view yourself in relation to others and your willingness to extend a helping hand to those in need. At some point, we must see ourselves as pillars of creation and creativity, individuals who recognize opportunities to do what is right.

You deeply value the idea of making the world a better place and not causing harm. You find true satisfaction in helping others, knowing that you also deserve a fulfilling life in the end. It's through these selfless actions that we gain the power to make a difference. It's important to realize that success doesn't happen overnight; it takes time and effort to reach a point where we can positively impact others' lives.

While it's not an everyday occurrence to have a heart that cares for many, your dedication to making a difference leads you to change lives daily. You could have chosen to be like everyone else, ignoring the world's problems, but you're driven by a deeper purpose beyond personal success. You live to experience fulfillment in every way, which can be challenging in a world where some lack empathy.

One might assume that achieving great things is easy, that you can simply dream something up and see it materialize the next day. However, this is rarely the case. Our universe is full of opportunities, and while there may be a problem that needs solving, others may also seek to capitalize on that same challenge.

So, when you venture out to make a difference, you might not always receive a warm welcome. You may encounter obstacles. Yet, if you truly love what you've become and believe it's your calling to see the world differently, you'll keep finding innovative ways to bring about change. While you may not be an advocate for human rights, consider yourself something more—a force for good in a world that needs it.

The gift can be quite challenging to explain because it's unique for each person and has a different meaning to the world and to you. Sometimes, you may discover a special talent or skill that can be used to help others, and this can become your path to achieving your dreams. It's important to remember that we all need to make a living, and this could be your way of contributing to the global community.

This can help you shine and stand out without having to compete with others or compromise your values. We are all individuals striving to accomplish things that capture everyone's attention because of our dedication and focus. Even if you're the first to understand life in a certain way, it's important not to look down on others. We should realize that our experiences create opportunities for others to follow their own paths, and by showing compassion, we can break free from unnecessary competition, where everyone is trying to correct one another.

Our unique abilities are incredibly important and can make a significant impact when used wisely. In a world with diverse perspectives, it's crucial not to underestimate the importance of striving for excellence, as some compromises cannot be undone. If you truly want to experience the magic within us all, keep an open mind and prioritize humanity in everything you do. You'll come to realize that a gift remains incomplete until you share it with others.

Our desires become real when we open our hearts to others. If you haven't given yourself fully, you may not understand your true self. People tend to accept what's good for them without questioning the world around them. When everything is going well, the spirit of curiosity that exists in everyone tends to fade. However, when a person compromises their true nature, they can become a force of rebellion. Don't underestimate the potential impact of such individuals.

Each of us is unique, and we learn a great deal along the way. One important lesson is the need to care for others. You have the ability to do amazing things. Love is a virtue that has built many empires, while its absence has caused harm to countless individuals and organizations. People can tell when they are being cared for and when they are not valued. You cannot deceive them into believing in something that isn't real.

So, don't just take from others; give a part of yourself, and you will receive in return. You may not fully understand the meaning of the saying, "It is better to give than to receive." If you only take from others, you will never have enough. It is through giving that we truly find our worth. Your role in life may not always require you to give, but it's not just about gaining or losing. It's about how we interact with each other that makes us human. Honoring the exchange of creation is what defines us.

With the unique gift you possess, you have the ability to touch the lives of countless people. It's not just about your performance as an artist or your involvement; it's about the genuine value you bring to everything you do. When you pursue what you love with the intention of making a positive impact on many lives, you can educate and inspire.

By doing so, you share a part of yourself, and it's evident that some of the things we do have a profound impact on others. Our world is filled with challenges, and not everyone is equally active or sees things the same way. This can leave many feeling powerless. However, when you reach out to humanity with genuine love and dedication in your endeavors, people can feel the compassion you have for them. This is where our focus should be when addressing the world's issues.

It's essential not to hide the truth, as authenticity shines through in everything you do. Be honest with people, guide them by sharing the real truths about who we are and what we can do to better understand ourselves. For many, this becomes the most significant platform for personal growth, a source of transformation that helps them navigate life's challenges. Through this kind of unwavering commitment, we can reach those who need us most. Offer the true essence of dedication, capable of changing lives, and help others discover their true selves.

People have the ability to have faith in your actions, and you've sown a seed of knowledge in someone's heart. This enables them to live with hope and positivity. Our purpose revolves around changing lives, and you shouldn't give up until you're sure you've provided people with what they desire most. You don't need to wander aimlessly across the world to connect with others. If you truly understand humanity, you know that they seek ways to comprehend their well-being.

We all know that no one can completely satisfy the longing to be human. As long as you're alive, you'll continue to seek a deeper understanding of life. Many people still depend on us because they want to grasp how to love each other more deeply, lead fulfilling lives, and increase their financial stability for their daily well-being. This also includes learning how to overcome the challenges that trouble them. You can never fully satisfy people's curiosity about life.

So, as you journey towards the limits of your understanding, remember that we are all in this together, needing each other's support. Encourage others to bring out their best selves and help them see life from a new perspective. Humans possess incredible talents, but sometimes, due to our circumstances, we lose sight of who we truly are. When you encounter someone who cares, they can guide you back to reality, and this is a sign of quality.

We all have expectations and desire the best for ourselves. This is how we gauge our existence in a normal world.

We measure the worth of our actions by our ability to make a positive impact on people's lives. Life can be complex, and we shouldn't let certain negative aspects go unchecked. Each of us faces challenges that can be very tough, and it's how we manage that pressure that reveals our character and dedication to serving humanity. Everyone experiences moments of deep sadness that can weigh them down or shatter their spirits, and how we respond to these moments sets us apart as extraordinary individuals.

We should strive to shield others from harmful experiences that we've encountered, understanding that these experiences won't benefit them. This is what earns us a special place in their hearts – our ability to absorb their pain. It's crucial to acknowledge that witnessing or experiencing certain things can be deeply distressing, and if this kind of life isn't suited to your nature, you might struggle to handle it. Despite the many factors that shape us, we must keep our hearts open to goodness because it's rare to find a world that genuinely cares.

You could have been anyone who has faced such harsh realities, and it may have caused irreparable damage inside you. Sometimes, we fail to comprehend the harshness of reality, but through our own experiences, we come to understand the importance of preventing such behavior from affecting all of humanity. If we were to accept everything as part of our reality, the world would become an unbearable place to live. Our minds can potentially harm others, but it's only when we allow external circumstances to dictate how we interpret what we've witnessed and how we respond that our true character is defined.

It is quite challenging to perceive the world as originally intended. Many alterations have occurred to cater to the specific needs of different individuals, and some aspects can never return to their original state. The process of modernization has significantly impacted our lives, perhaps going too far. Rectifying such matters often necessitates considerable sacrifice, pushing one's limits beyond comprehension. To truly understand, you must have lived and experienced it. No one is inherently destined to guide others through life's trials, and no one should be sacrificed for self-discovery.

Imagine finding yourself on such a unique path, where our individual roles in the world are impossible to replicate, and articulating them proves elusive for others to grasp. Despite our efforts to shield people from reality, there may come a time when we must elucidate our evolving nature. As life progresses, the complexities of our inner thoughts mount, and art alone is insufficient to connect with the world. We must invent new means of communication.

You can never fully grasp the struggles others are enduring, as most are preoccupied with their immediate circumstances. However, if you find contentment in the components that shape our daily lives, you can begin to comprehend the world around you. So, don't underestimate yourself if you navigate this intricate world, dealing with phenomena unfamiliar to many, yet potentially pivotal. Understand that when challenges intensify, many surrender hope in anticipation of a brighter future beyond the present turmoil.

Perhaps, in the future, we can discover many solutions even when we face failure. This can help us understand why sometimes we don't get what we deserve. Often, we find ourselves stuck between the present and the future, struggling to see things clearly. This can lead to a lot of pain and disappointment when our hopes don't pan out. It's tough to understand why things go wrong, especially when we go through such experiences.

Sometimes, we lack the persistence needed to achieve our goals. We need to remember that things can change, even when we're holding onto the past. Eventually, you may come to realize your purpose in life.

When you find something special about yourself, hold onto it and take pride in it. Understand that not everyone discovers who they truly are. Many people fail to understand themselves, not because they don't know what they're doing, but because they don't possess your unique gift. You should cherish your unique ideas and values.

Don't let anything come between you and your ability to understand things. Your self-awareness is incredibly valuable, and it defines your true worth. Even when life gets tough, remember who you are and what you've always wanted. This knowledge can protect you from many challenges along the way.

In our lives, we encounter various situations. It's important to handle them with genuine knowledge. People often judge us by our character, especially when we face tough times. Sometimes, it's tempting to conform to the world's expectations, but you should embrace who you are.

You should understand and accept yourself as you are. Don't worry too much about how others became who they are. Focus on what works for you and makes life simpler. Keep these principles close to your heart. When things don't go as planned, remember how to stand up for yourself. Embrace diversity; you are unique, and you don't have to conform to everyone else's ideas.

Sometimes, sticking to your own way of thinking may seem challenging, but it's not. It's about becoming the person you aspire to be. You need to believe in yourself and have the strength to overcome obstacles. We often hold onto things that serve no purpose, and pressure can make us feel like we should conform. However, to truly discover yourself, you need a strong backbone that can withstand challenges. This is how you reveal your true self.

The past can be like a heavy weight pulling you down, but you are not defined by your past. You are the future, full of untapped potential. You must believe in your ability to change things for the better. Have faith in the part of you that will bring about positive transformations. Don't let external influences change who you are.

There are forces in life that may try to shape you according to their desires. Stay true to yourself and your vision. You are on a journey to create a new world, one that hasn't been seen or experienced yet. This belief in your potential is crucial.

Remember, what's dragging you down is your past, but you are the future. Believe in your power to shape your destiny and resist being molded into something you're not.

If you let the experiences you face change you, who will guide your dreams, the things you truly want to witness, things that are too precious to entrust to anyone else? So, have faith in yourself. Even when faced with tough challenges, don't let your potential wither away. When you give your all and it still feels like it's not enough, remember that your efforts aren't in vain. They are building within you, shaping who you are.

It would be unfortunate to lose sight of ourselves like that. There must be a reason behind all the hard work we put into pursuing our deepest desires. However, in the world we inhabit, one must always be vigilant. There might be people out there with ulterior motives, ready to take advantage of your dedication, which can be soul-crushing.

So, how do you prepare for the challenges that lie ahead, knowing that the world can be unforgiving, and many things can go awry? Despite these obstacles, you have a singular goal: to seize that once-in-a-lifetime opportunity to apply your knowledge. You don't have to compromise; you simply step out into the world, revealing your true self and your capabilities. No matter how tough it gets, no matter the difficulties and hurdles along the journey, you keep your focus on what sets you apart.

In life, you never really know who might try to bring you down or spot potential in the person you've evolved into. Even though people might have faced numerous challenges, there's always a chance you could be pushed back to where you started. Therefore, when you embark on your journey, make sure you're not only prepared for your aspirations but also resilient enough to resist external forces that may attempt to manipulate you.

Understand that true fulfillment doesn't come until you reach your destination and fully embrace your identity. You are not just a small entity in this vast universe; we exist to create history, and perhaps you can leave your lasting legacy, gaining recognition beyond your wildest dreams. The catch is that unwavering dedication is a rare quality in an ordinary world.

Chapter Sixteen

Moment of glory

You should not always underestimate yourself. It's important to recognize when you've done your part adequately and take joy in it, as this is what truly matters. This happens when you've been working hard to achieve something meaningful to you, regardless of the challenges you face. Your primary goal becomes committing to something worthy of your efforts, and when you reach the end, you've accomplished everything as planned.

Despite periods of confusion and self-doubt, you navigated through challenges without a clear direction for a long time. Your own choices had limited your world, making it challenging to achieve what you envisioned. It's remarkable how much effort goes into aligning yourself with your aspirations. Sometimes, it's essential to find solutions in every situation, as this greatly impacts your life. Discovering these solutions becomes your only way to regain normality.

Initially, you might have believed that things would be easier from your perspective, but reality often questions your assumptions. You may find yourself locked in confusion, wondering if you'll ever grasp what's expected of you. Sometimes, when we're too certain about our actions from a distance, we realize that we're standing with no clear path to achieving our goals. This is especially true when we're limited to our own perspective, unaware of the outside world's complexity.

You once aspired to be the answer to many questions, even though you didn't fully understand the causes. Now that you're deeply engaged in life, you've come to realize that good intentions alone can't make things as easy as you once thought. To make a real difference, you must be more than just an advocate or a voice for humanity; you must become part of the solution.

Yes, you aspire to be significant by doing something unique and different. However, now the focus has expanded, and you find yourself at the center of it all. You possess a deep understanding of things, and you believe you can accomplish remarkable feats that would amaze people. But what truly matters now is what lies within you. It's the inner voice, the lifelong aspiration you've come to recognize and understand. You've identified its meaning, its purpose, and how you can turn it into reality.

Considering all the time that has passed, you are certain that this is the moment to share your gifts with the world, to be understood fully, and you cannot accept anything less. Whatever you've done to reach this point must suffice, for it's about the journey from then until now, and you are confident that you've given your best effort. Your goal is to stand out, and your intentions are pure. Achieving that level of distinction is about being entirely different, and you embrace this uniqueness as a positive trait.

You may have nurtured this aspiration silently, but a small part of you still harbors doubt. You realize that if you can reach that pinnacle, it would mark a once-in-a-lifetime historical moment in your life. It's the moment when you aim to stand tall and change a part of reality as we know it. Whether others comprehend your mission or not, we are all here to make positive things happen. Once you set your mind to it, you cannot remain unnoticed.

Your journey has been unconventional, filled with challenges that weren't easy to grasp. You've left behind a previous life, and while you might try to conceal it, you can't truly be content without sharing your knowledge. So, if you're fortunate, the moment you've long awaited for may come soon. You've been diligently preparing yourself for this opportunity, constantly improving from where you began. You recognize that the key lies within you, and you carry yourself with confidence, knowing that doing it correctly can bring you immense pride.

When you've thoroughly prepared yourself, patiently anticipating that rare opportunity to step boldly into the realm of knowledge, it's the moment you've been eagerly waiting for, a moment that stretches your memory back to your very essence as a human being. You've diligently honed your talents, arming yourself to the hilt to embody the very essence of excellence. It takes just one opportunity, one chance, to forever alter the course of your life. This is the pivotal juncture that flings wide open the doors to a dimension of creation that has always danced in the recesses of your dreams. All that preparation, all that effort, all those hours dedicated to perfecting your craft, they all converge at this precise juncture – an opportunity so seldom encountered.

Thus, you dedicate your entire existence to the pursuit of your deepest passion, and you find no room for boredom because you remain blissfully ignorant of the vastness with which the world can unfurl before you. Unlike our origins, in this new chapter of creation, we don't exist by mere happenstance; rather, we thrive through the sheer might of our capabilities. We toil day in and day out, our daily exertions accumulating like precious currency, for they constitute the bedrock of our aspirations. Certainty eludes us until destiny's embrace, as we are compelled to question the true extent of our learnings and how far our fervor and daily horizons have taken us. Whether we deem it essential or not, we are the kind of individuals wholly reliant on our well-honed skills and our ability to bring our dreams into tangible existence in order to find our footing in the ordinary.

Regardless of whether we were schooled or arrived at our understanding independently, every endeavor demands an unwavering commitment to self-improvement. The relentless pursuit of excellence remains the universal prerequisite for reaching one's desired destination. In the relentless pursuit of your craft, as you immerse yourself deeply in all that you've come to know, it is from this wellspring that greatness emerges. Perfection does not manifest overnight; it demands the passage of time, the valor to confront challenges, and the resilience to attain precision. Eventually, you reach a juncture where you are called upon to exhibit the fruits of your labor over time. Understand that you cannot possibly grasp every facet of existence; thus, you must be willing to engage in introspection, to refine your understanding. This is the journey of the stars, individuals eternally striving for perfection, and it's what you will ultimately cherish about yourself – that your relentless efforts have transformed you into something remarkable.

Discovering the true worth of self-driven effort becomes evident when you find yourself in a situation where you must showcase all that you've acquired.

Our potential is not boundless, but when we navigate this phase of life with care, we can reach remarkable heights. So, never retreat, for you never know when an opportunity will arise where you must perform extraordinary feats. Such chances are rare and define your significance. We have much to live for and aspire to be, and embracing this path signifies recognizing your place in the creative realm.

Imagine the incredible transformation possible when you seize every opportunity with enthusiasm and a desire to grow. Why is it seemingly effortless for some? The outcome of your life rests in your hands, as only you control its direction. A gateway to your desires lies within, and you possess the keys to unlock it. You hold the power to excel when you actively seek it.

When you've observed the world, felt its call, and chosen to understand it independently, you've embarked on a courageous journey. You have the potential to thrive, so don't let it slip away. Your unique talents can make a profound statement about your comprehension. Embrace the gift of the moment, which aligns with your lifelong passion. Fulfill your role in various capacities, excelling in at least one, for each of us possesses a distinctive strength.

Even if you tend towards laziness, there's an area where diligence can shine through. Find the courage to persist in pursuing your passions. Unless you've decided that creation holds no allure, remember that withholding your potential only hinders your own life. The abilities reside within you; you must cultivate the discipline to manifest your deepest desires. Strength and potential dwell within; your love can become your reality through consistent effort.

What's behind the door could be your greatest achievement, and it's all within your reach. When you're fully prepared, you get one chance to make a strong first impression. You might wonder about yourself, your purpose, and whether you're living a meaningful life. Trying to live in two worlds without proper preparation can lead to distractions, costing you your focus and potential.

Struggling to be recognized and waiting for opportunities is one thing, but giving up entirely is another. Even if you try to convince yourself otherwise, not trying at all leaves you feeling invisible and full of regret. Hard work helps us discover our talents and take pride in our achievements. Life may not unfold exactly as expected, but it's a journey that shapes you from within.

You could have chosen to stay in the shadows, but embracing your talents can heal you and transform your identity. Discovering your unique abilities allows you to break free from limitations and become a part of creation. Wherever you are headed, let the universe express itself through you. Strive for something more, and question whether you're living your purpose. Until you find your true desire, you may feel incomplete.

Find meaning and a solution in the freedom that life offers. Your purpose becomes magnificent when you pay attention to your goals. Life doesn't pause with your attempts; it keeps moving forward. Greatness awaits you, and when you've given your best, don't be afraid. You didn't live in vain; you lived to discover your true worth on this challenging journey, just like everyone else who faces fears and obstacles along the way.

Sometimes, you might find yourself feeling a bit tired of tomorrow when you wake up and realize that you haven't achieved anything noteworthy. Many things may still be the same, and you're in the same place where you started. A fully lived life isn't just about preparing for the next day; it's about preparing for your entire existence. You're evolving into a new and better version of yourself, and greatness is becoming a part of who you are. It's happening faster than you might expect, every time you put in effort to shape your destiny.

We are capable of more than we often acknowledge. It's important to be content with ourselves and find effective ways to demonstrate our abilities. It's crucial to be precise when giving your best. Challenges will arise, but it becomes much tougher when you're unsure of your goals. Avoid reaching a point where you're not succeeding because you haven't discovered your true self. Remember that you possess immense potential, and everything you do is fueled by that potential. You have knowledge beyond what you may realize.

Opportunities don't come every day, so seize them when they do. Behind every successful person is someone with a dream and a goal they want to be known for. Make the most of every moment you're given, knowing that it didn't come easily and that it was one of the most challenging obstacles you had to overcome. If you believe in yourself, you can achieve anything you desire. You can reach the pinnacle of success, but only if you've put in the effort. You can't always buy your way to success; you have to earn it.

Something special will emerge within you when you stand by what you know. You can't possibly know everything, and that's okay – it's a universal agreement. But strive to learn enough to have a fulfilling life. Our existence offers us limited chances, and some may even doubt our connection to success. Failure shapes us profoundly, yet we hold onto the belief that we deserve a chance at life. That's our aspiration: an opportunity to redefine our self-perceptions. We march forward with doubts in our hearts, only to start believing when our goals take shape. No matter how daunting or improbable things seem, we must establish trust in ourselves.

With this comprehension, your thirst for knowledge can never be quenched. You are the missing teacher within, capable of transforming everything into art. How can you truly appreciate yourself if you've never discovered your distinctive qualities or taken pride in your individuality? There's so much about us, about others, and about life that remains unknown, but it must come alive through your dedication to love.

We must maximize the life we've been given; it's a quintessential human pursuit. If you fail to demonstrate this about yourself, you risk losing your sense of integrity. It's a crucial juncture in your life journey that should never be doubted. Think about the struggle we all face in finding meaning, despite the immense potential we possess as human beings. There's always a toll to pay before reaching the victorious destination on the other side. So, persevere, never tire of doing what you love, and reach the point where your hard work satisfies your inner drive.

A moment will come that will forever transform your essence, all because you altered your perspective on many aspects of life.

It only takes a single opportunity to transform your entire being, and this transformation is independent of how others perceive you. When you triumph from within, external influences hold no sway over you. Consider this moment as the birth of your greatest era, a time during which you may have waited longer than you ever desired or even throughout your entire life. This period is as beautiful as the countless times you've relished its glory in solitude. Nevertheless, the ultimate judgment of everything will occur on that fateful day, and the verdict will be rendered based on your merit.

You can love and cherish something deeply, but you may have never imagined that one day it would be the sole treasure nestled close to your heart, granting newfound purpose. The milestones in your life, the journey from humble beginnings to the point of transformation, all converge here. Bear in mind that the world won't present you with gifts; you must seize opportunities and employ them wisely, turning your gaze away from distractions, for they serve no other purpose. Deep within that realm where you emerged is where you truly belong.

If you've cultivated your inner self, nothing can obstruct your path to that coveted goal. It will inevitably materialize in the near or distant future, revealing your ever-expanding capabilities as you work diligently day by day. This potential isn't merely skin-deep; it emanates from your core. You possess a kind of magic, and all you need is faith and belief to bring it to life. Through this inner strength, you can conquer and dispel all external negative forces, making your inner radiance visible to all.

Discover the true essence of contentment and the art of living confidently. Although it may seem challenging, having unwavering faith is the key to unlocking a new world, one that has always been your cherished dream. You possess the strength to conquer every obstacle that has diminished your spirit in the past. Don't wait for others to guide you; seize this pivotal moment to transform into the person you truly love and aspire to be.

As you accumulate knowledge and experience the passage of time, the sacrifices you've made become a testament to your resilience. It should be abundantly clear that no one can stand in the way of your destiny. While your eagerness for change may be palpable, remember that change requires action. To bring out the best within you, summon your commitment to hard work and confront the challenges that have long evaded resolution. Transform your dreams from mere fantasies into tangible realities, fully aware that such transformations seldom occur without effort.

This is the era to redefine your perception of yourself. Time has concealed your potential for far too long, acting like a mask that obscures your true self from the world. Your aspirations can only manifest through unyielding determination. When you nurture your inner vision, remain steadfast, and never avert your gaze from your deepest desires, you harness the power within you. We are all individuals on a journey of self-discovery, learning and growing through our unique abilities. While progress may be temporarily hindered, it ultimately depends on what you seek to comprehend and achieve in this ever-evolving world.

Some things may seem complicated at times, but remember, your goal is within reach. Don't let doubt cloud your vision; many people make that mistake when pursuing their dreams. Sometimes, they overlook the true significance of their aspirations and the potential benefits they can bring. They fail to recognize their own power to surpass expectations. Why not you? Why shouldn't you be the one to achieve it? Ultimately, you are the one who understands how to be your best self.

In any situation you encounter, you can find a way forward when you tap into your inner strength. You are the protagonist in your life's story, and victory is within your grasp. When you feel a lack of motivation to pursue your passions, remember that your heart holds the potential to fulfill your deepest dreams. It's disheartening to depend on others to realize your goals. If you continue to rely on external sources to achieve what you're fully capable of accomplishing on your own, your success remains in a distant world. You have the power to reach that world independently.

Embrace the idea of being self-reliant and adventurous, knowing it's the cornerstone of life, leading to endless possibilities. If you're uncertain why it's essential, consider that successful individuals have walked this path before you. They followed their unique journeys and persisted in their pursuit of greatness. The only time you may lack courage is when you haven't recognized its significance. Deep within your heart, you must discover your motivation, and it should be compelling enough to drive you forward. Have faith in your abilities, unwaveringly and with greater conviction each day. Remember, you are embarking on a journey that stretches to the limits of your existence, and challenges are an inherent part of this magnificent adventure.

You're doing something that many people think is impossible to achieve, and it can be confusing for many until you decide to take control. Believe in this more than anything else, knowing it will always be there to support you. No matter what challenges you face, your talent will be there to protect you, even when you feel trapped. Your dedication will ultimately set you free. Concentrate deeply and keep growing until you break the chains that seem to hold you down.

The issues you're complaining about now are largely of your own making. You might lament that you never had a chance, but you can start building your chances of success now. Yes, opportunities will come your way, but it's up to you to make the most of them. The world out there is vast, and you might feel lost in unfamiliar territory. However, you can always understand your own creations and never be lost again.

We all have our unique stories to tell. Our love lives are like little soap operas, filled with the challenges of loving and finding true love. Our passions and interests are like songs we constantly sing, and our lives are like movies where we are the stars. There are obstacles and challenges along the way, but with determination, you can overcome them.

There's always that one thing, your greatest fear, that can seem insurmountable and block your path. It stands in the way of everything you do, but with enough preparation and effort, you can conquer that challenging part of your journey. You can achieve everything you deserve, because whether you like it or not, whether you give up or keep going, success will always be within your reach.

So, let's remember something important once again: never close your eyes to your dreams. Don't get bored or tired of working hard to achieve what you truly desire. Be honest with yourself about your desires, and deep inside, you already possess everything you need to reach the pinnacle of success. Don't assume that if you lose focus, the worst can't happen. It can, just as much as the best can become a reality. Stay focused and face challenges head-on.

This could be your one chance to live freely. Life comes with duties, and you don't want to neglect yours indefinitely. Deep within yourself, you only need to break free from that self-imposed limitation that keeps you living in fear. The real truth is, your dreams won't come true without giving your all to them.

Live to embrace your unique talents. You can achieve what others might not even imagine possible. Your goals can only be realized when you wholeheartedly commit to them. No matter what you dream about, you can make it a reality because the answers have always been within you. You're the one with the power to answer your own prayers, so don't give up on anything, including your own aspirations, because you'll bring them to fruition.

You have the ability to manifest your deepest desires. The greatest power to turn your dreams and goals into reality resides within you. Imagine what you can achieve when you have the support of your faith. Your desires are heard, and the universe awaits your action. For what it's worth, there's nothing you can't become if you fully dedicate yourself to it. Don't waste time convincing others; prove to yourself that you're capable.

The End!!!

About the Author

Sibusiso Malvin Tshabangu Born 7 October 1986, South Africa. Studied at the Tshwane University Of Technology with a B Tech: Degree In Marketing. My books are solely based on my research which I have conducted for over twelve years, after completing my studies, which I later had a breakthrough in Pharmaceutical studies, which became my area of practice, however choose to focus mainly on life and relationships as a reflection of my understanding, which emphasizes on the fact that to avoid a lot of what we can define as diseases and medical disorders, man and woman should learn to focus on love, even if you can be a Master in life, on its own knowledge cannot do that much, love completes everything that we are.

Other Books by the Author

1. Inspiration About Life or Love

<u>*2 The Series Stars Do Fall in Love*</u>

1. Individualism

2. Fame

3. The Lady at the Center of my Heart